**Prentice Hall
train &
assess it
generation**

The information you will need:

1. The Access Code for PH Train & Assess IT, found in your packaging.

   Write that Access Code here:

   _____

2. A Course/Section code that your instructor will provide.

   Write that course/section code here:

   _____

Editor-in-Chief: Natalie Anderson
Executive Editor: Jodi McPherson
Editorial Assistant: Alana Meyers
Media Project Manager: Joan Waxman
Manager, Print Production: Christy Mahon
Production Editor & Buyer: Wanda Rockwell
Composition: Digital Content Factory Ltd.
Cover Printer: Phoenix Color Corp.
Interior Printer & Binder: Courier, Inc.

Microsoft Excel, Solver, and Windows are registered trademarks of Microsoft Corporation in the U.S.A. and other countries. Screen shots and icons reprinted with permission from the Microsoft Corporation. This book is not sponsored or endorsed by or affiliated with Microsoft Corporation.

Copyright © 2005 by Pearson Education, Inc., Upper Saddle River, New Jersey, 07458.
Pearson Prentice Hall. All rights reserved. Printed in the United States of America. This publication is protected by Copyright and permission should be obtained from the publisher prior to any prohibited reproduction, storage in a retrieval system, or transmission in any form or by any means, electronic, mechanical, photocopying, recording, or likewise. For information regarding permission(s), write to: Rights and Permissions Department.

Pearson Prentice Hall[TM] is a trademark of Pearson Education, Inc.

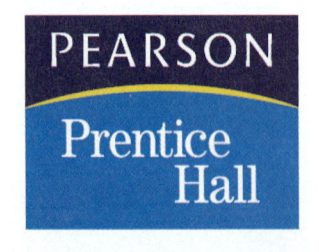

10 9 8 7 6 5 4 3 2 1
ISBN 0-13-148846-5

Prentice Hall's - Train & Assess IT Contents

Train & Assess IT Overview

Systems Requirements 1

Installing Authorware 1

Attention AOL Users: 1

Installing the Partial Local Install (PLI) CD 2
   Installing the PLI: 2

Web Only Access 7
   Installing the Macromedia Authorware plug-in for Internet Explorer from
   the Train & Assess IT Website: 7
   Installing the Macromedia Authorware plug-in for Netscape from
   the Train & Assess IT Website: 10
   Logging into to Train & Assess IT for the first time.. 15
   Student Self-Registration 15
   Registering with an Assigned Student Account.. 19

Navigating Around Train & Assess IT

Train & Assess IT Main Menu 23
   User Guides 23
      Training Guide 23
      Testing Guide 23
      Student Guide 24
   My Modules 24
   My Statistics 24
   My Messages 24
   Glossary 24
   Change Password 25
   Sign Out 25
   Contact Professor.. 26
   Contact Tech Support 26

Training Walkthrough Overview 27
   Begin a Training Lesson... 27
   Navigate and Use Training... 28

Assessment Walkthrough Overview 31
   Navigate and Use Assessment 32

Tech Support 36

Uninstalling the Partial Local Install CD 37
   Uninstalling the Partial Local Install CD 37

The Train IT CD 39

Installing the Partial Local Install (PLI) CD

In order to make the installation process for the PLI an easy one, please be aware of the following:

- The PLI should NOT be installed on or run from your network server, but rather will need to be installed on each individual workstation's hard drive. Instructors: Please use available technology in your labs to ensure each desktop is loaded with the PLI.
- Permission Level for the PHIT Folder: Once the PLI is installed, students need to be able to have write/modify permissions to all items within the PH Train & Assess IT Folder (in Program Files folder). Please ensure this is done after the installation process.

Note: *If you are installing the PLI on Windows NT, Windows 2000, or Windows XP, you may need to speak with your network administrator to properly install the software because of access restrictions.*

❖ INSTALL PROCEDURE

Installing the PLI:

1. Insert the **PLI CD** into CD-ROM drive.
   The InstallShield Wizard will automatically open up.

2. Click on **Next**.

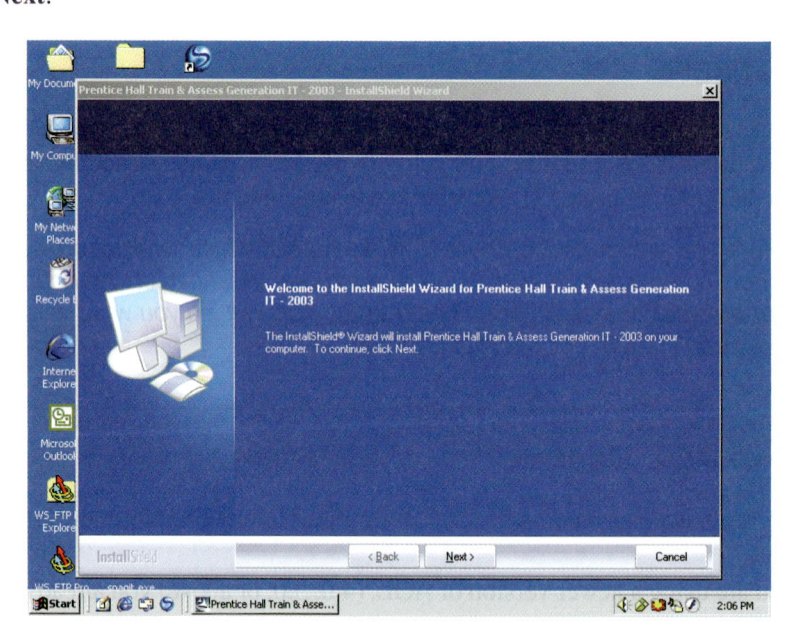

Installing the Partial Local Install (PLI) CD (Cont'd)

3. Read the license agreement and click **Yes**.

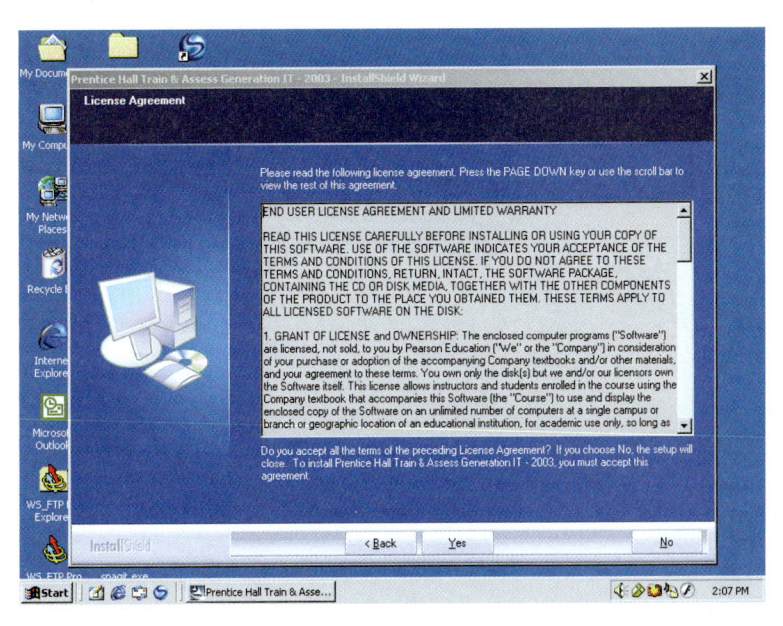

4. A destination folder has already been selected for you. However, if you want to install to a different folder, click **Browse** and select another folder.

5. Click **Next**.

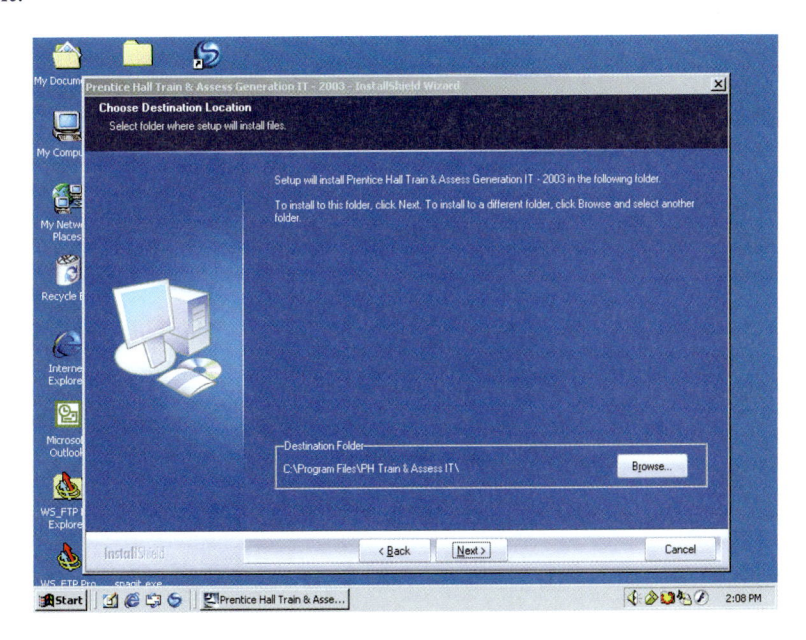

Installing the Partial Local Install (PLI) CD (Cont'd)

6. Select the training, testing, or both.

7. Click **Next**.

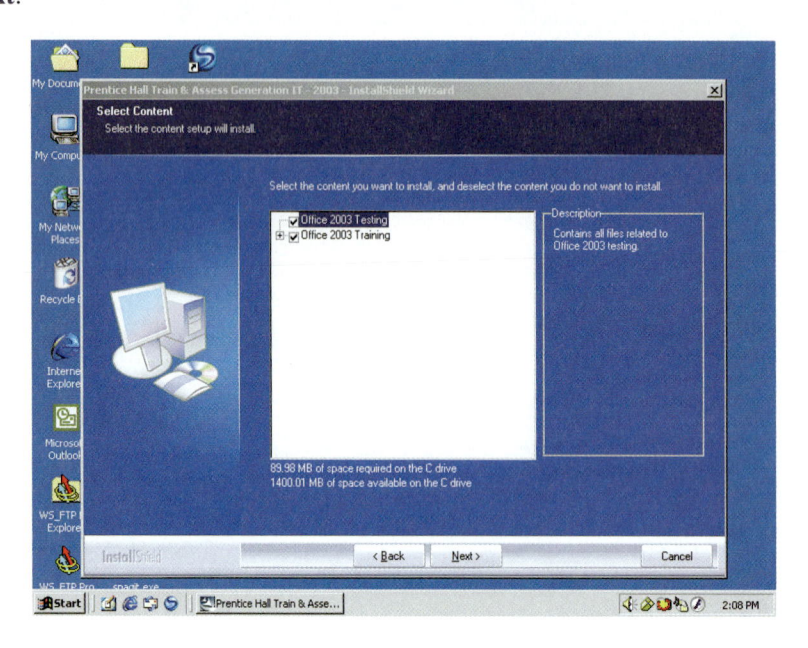

8. Make sure the Web site address is **http://www.phgenit.com**.

9. Click **Next**.

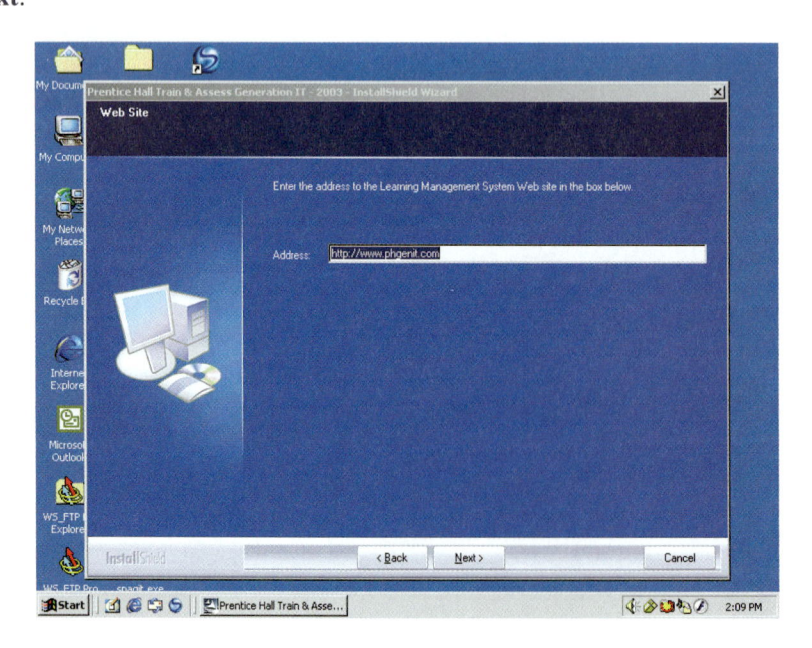

Installing the Partial Local Install (PLI) CD (Cont'd)

10. You will be asked if you would like to create a desktop icon. Click **Yes**.

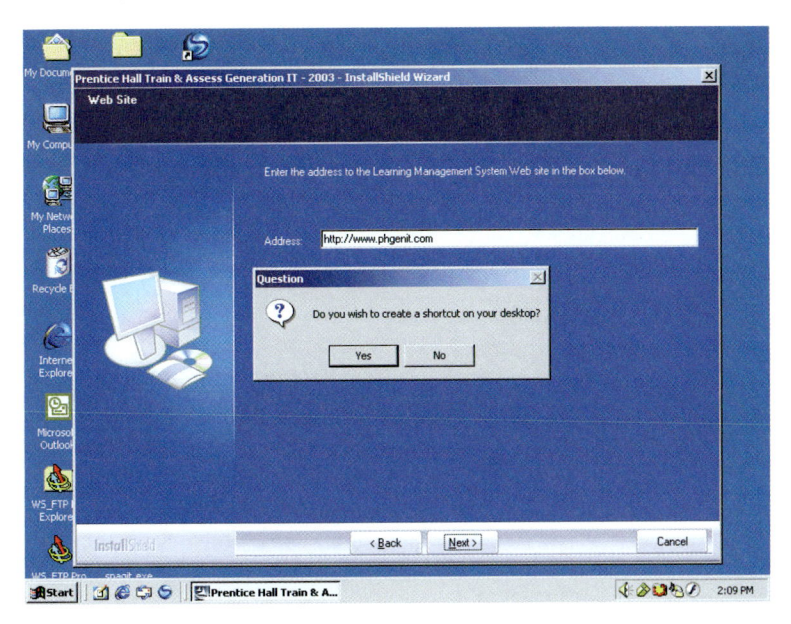

11. Setup is now ready to copy files.
12. Click **Next**.

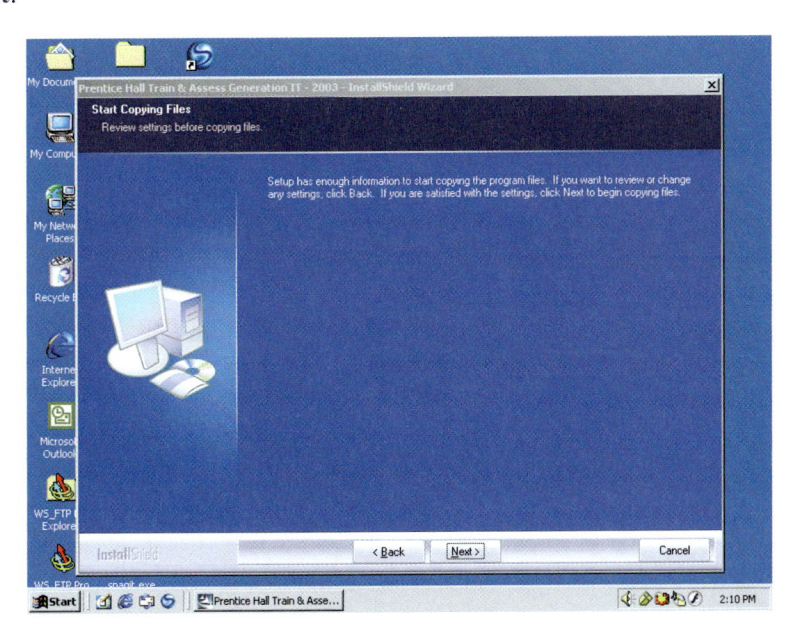

Installing the Partial Local Install (PLI) CD (Cont'd)

13. Once the installation has completed successfully, click on **Finish**.

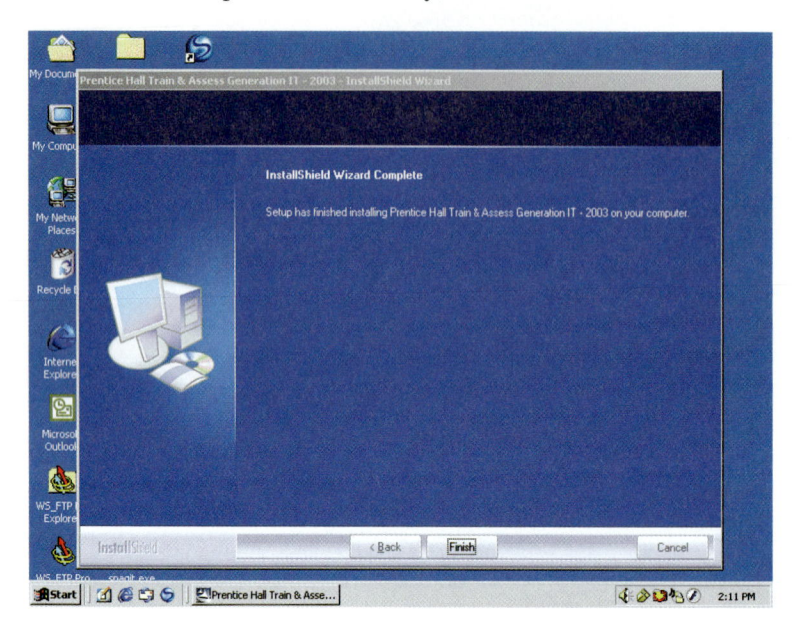

14. To begin using Train and Assess IT, click on the **PHIT** icon on your desktop.

❖❖❖

Web Only Access

The following installation procedures are required only when using Train & Assess IT on the Web.

❖ INSTALL PROCEDURE

Installing the Macromedia Authorware plug-in for Internet Explorer from the Train & Assess IT Website:

1. Go to: **http://www.phgenit.com.**

2. Click on the blue button at the bottom the screen that says "GET AUTHORWARE WEBPLAYER".

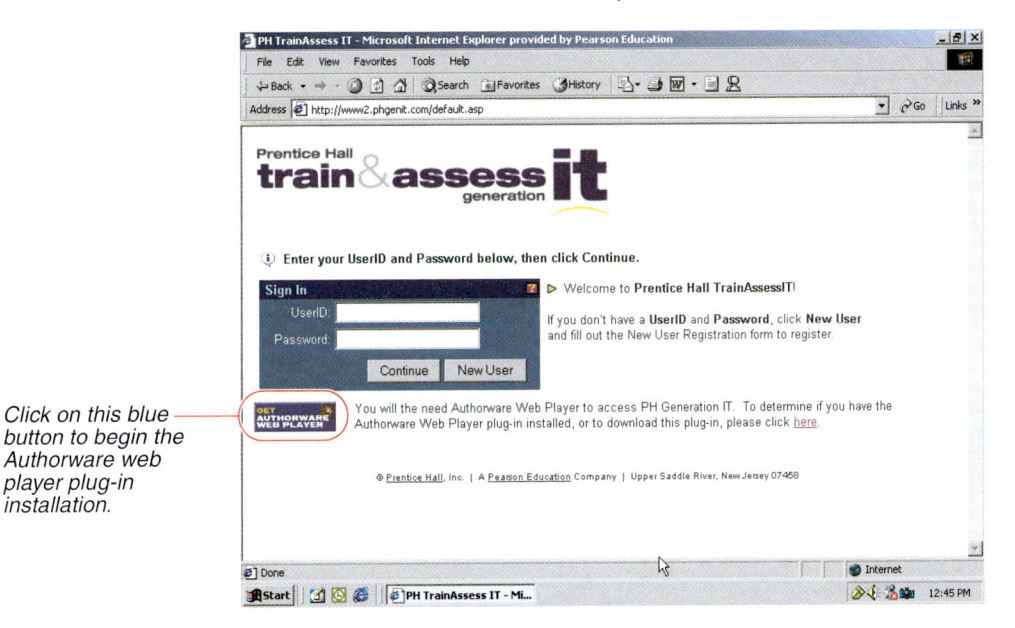

Click on this blue button to begin the Authorware web player plug-in installation.

7

Web Only Access (Cont'd)

3. Clicking on the blue button will cause the program installer to begin the Authorware installation. If the installer detects you are running Internet Explorer, it will begin the Authorware Web Player plug-in install automatically.

If there is not a Macromedia logo in this window yet, it means that the Authorware install is not complete. Normally you need to wait a few minutes for the install to complete. Do not exit.

4. After waiting a few minutes (wait-time varies depending on the speed of your connection; 56K modem connections are estimated to take 11 minutes to complete the install), you will get a Security Warning asking you for permission to run the Authorware Web Player control. This installs the plug-in you need to access the program training and testing content. You must click on **Yes** for the install to be successful.

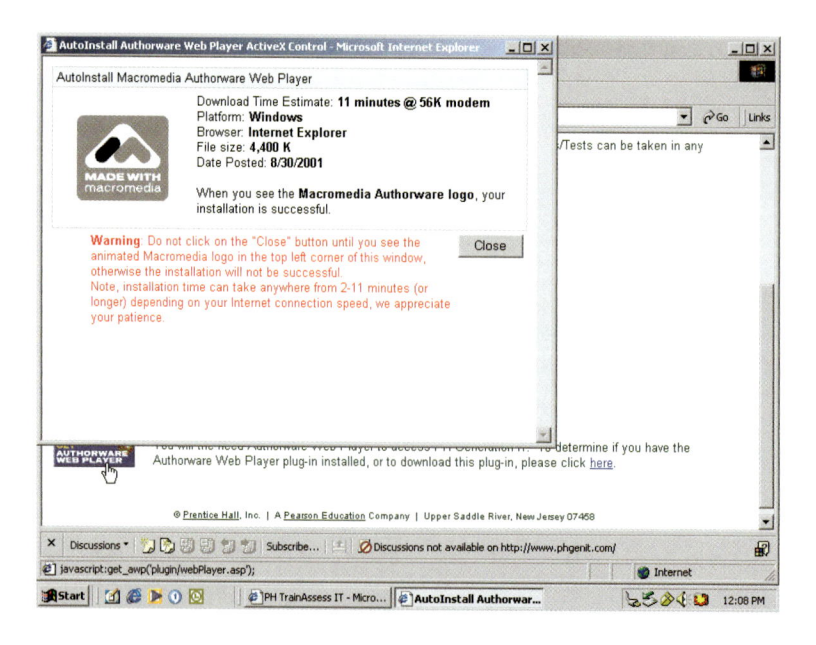

Web Only Access (Cont'd)

5. Shortly after you accept the warning above you will see the following screen:

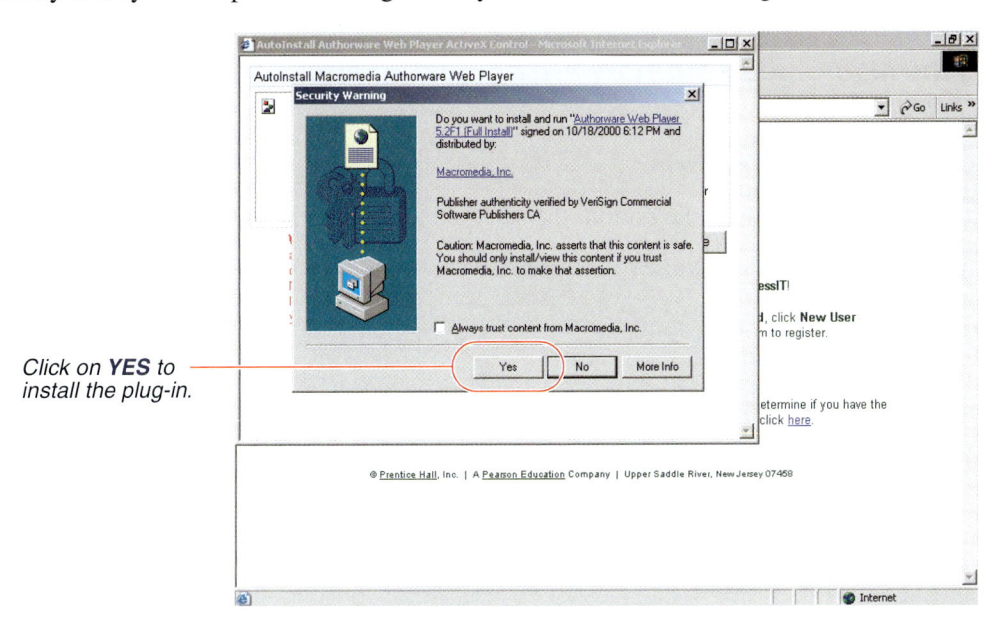

*Click on **YES** to install the plug-in.*

6. The install of the plug-in is successful as soon as you see the following screen, which should come up after the screen above. Please note the wavy line.

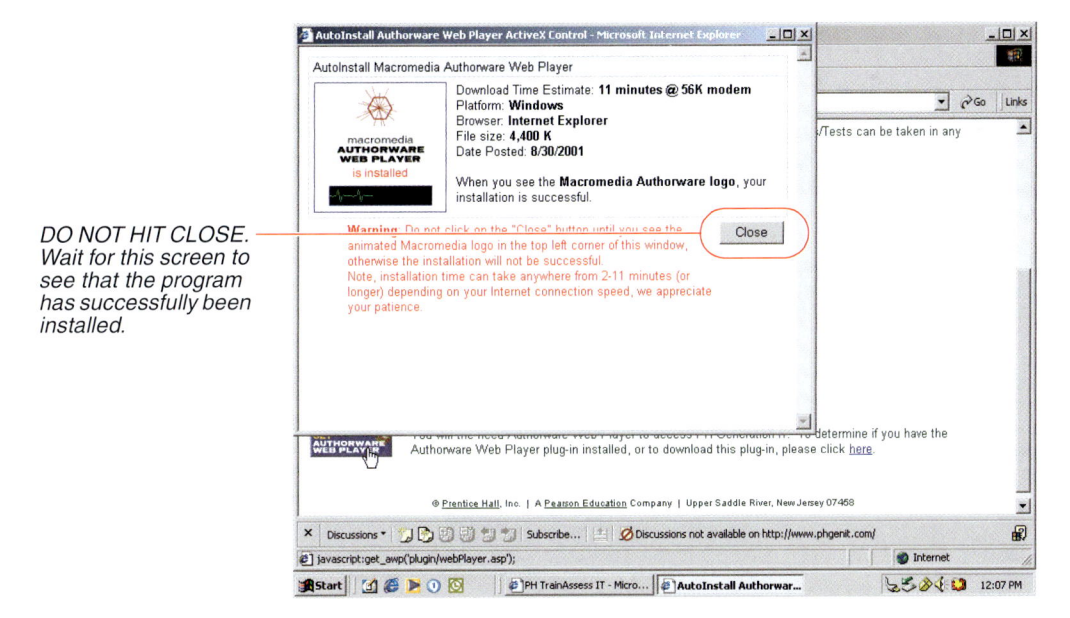

DO NOT HIT CLOSE. Wait for this screen to see that the program has successfully been installed.

7. Finally, click on the **Close** button at the bottom of the window and log into the program to begin your training or testing.

❖❖❖

Web Only Access (Cont'd)

❖ INSTALL PROCEDURE

Installing the Macromedia Authorware plug-in for **Netscape** *from the Train & Assess IT Website:*

1. Go to: **http://www.phgenit.com**.

2. Click on the blue button at the bottom the screen that says "GET AUTHORWARE WEBPLAYER".

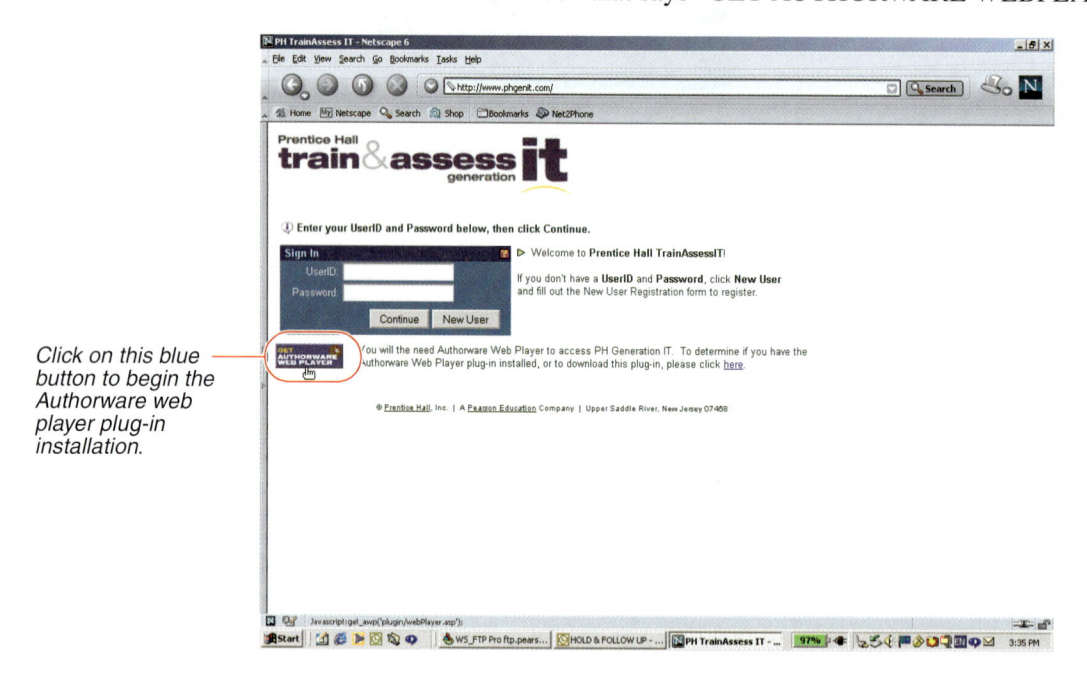

Click on this blue button to begin the Authorware web player plug-in installation.

Web Only Access (Cont'd)

3. Clicking on the blue button will display instructions for downloading the installer for the Netscape version of the plug-in.

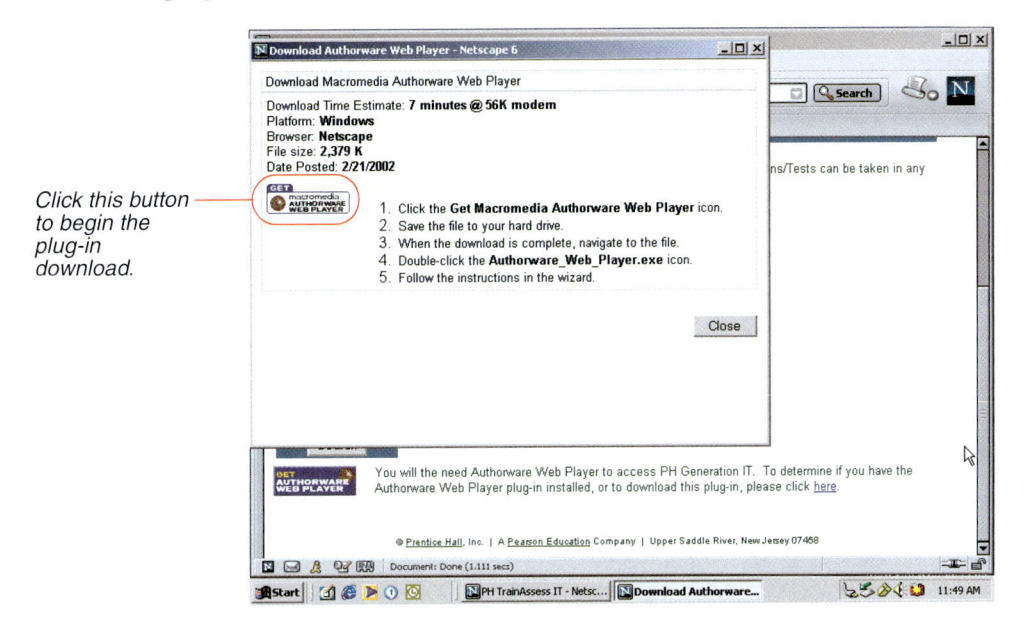

Click this button to begin the plug-in download.

4. A window will pop-up, prompting you to save the installer you are downloading to a specific location. Make a note of the directory to which you are saving the installer. You will need to find it to begin the install. It is easiest to save it to your Desktop.

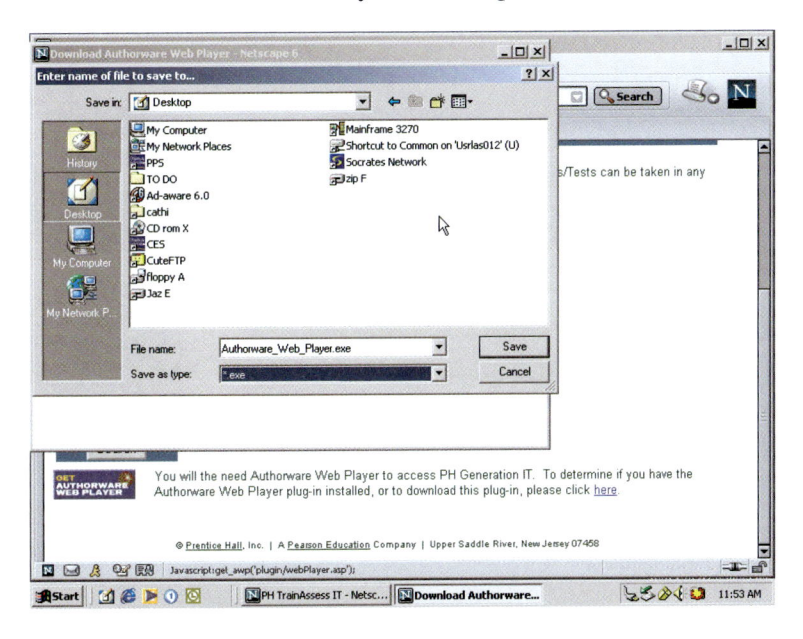

Web Only Access (Cont'd)

5. Once the **Authorware_Web_Player.exe** file is finished saving, locate the file you downloaded and double click on it to begin the install. If you installed it to the Desktop, locate the icon on your desktop and double click on it.

6. Once the install starts you will see the installation wizard below. Click on **Next** to continue.

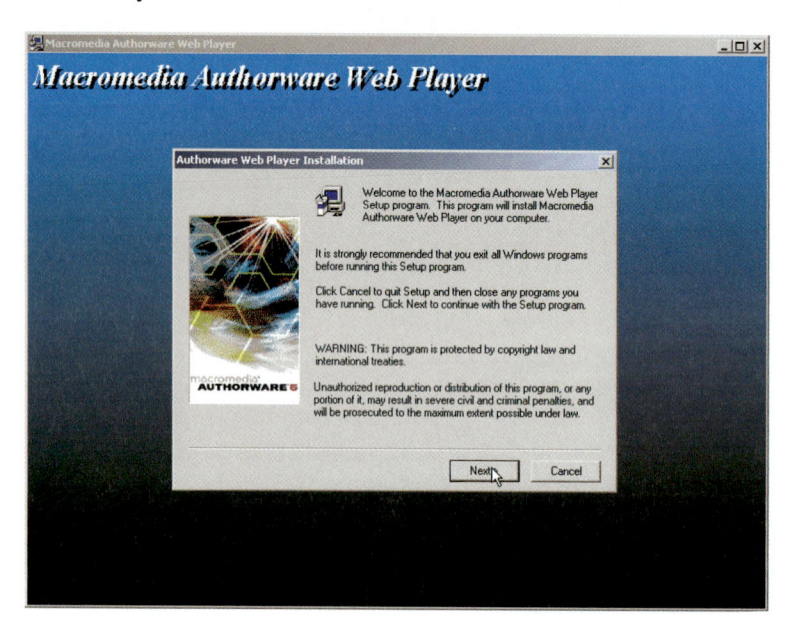

7. You will now see the license agreement. You must click **Yes** to continue the installation. Clicking **No** will exit you out of the program.

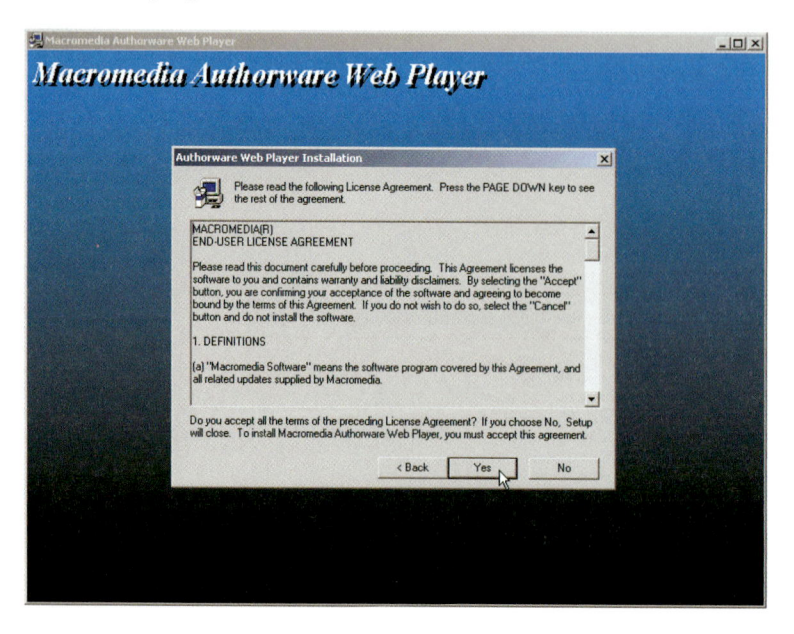

Web Only Access (Cont'd)

8. Specify your browser from the list of available browsers. Make sure you highlight and select your version of **Netscape**, and then click on **Next**.

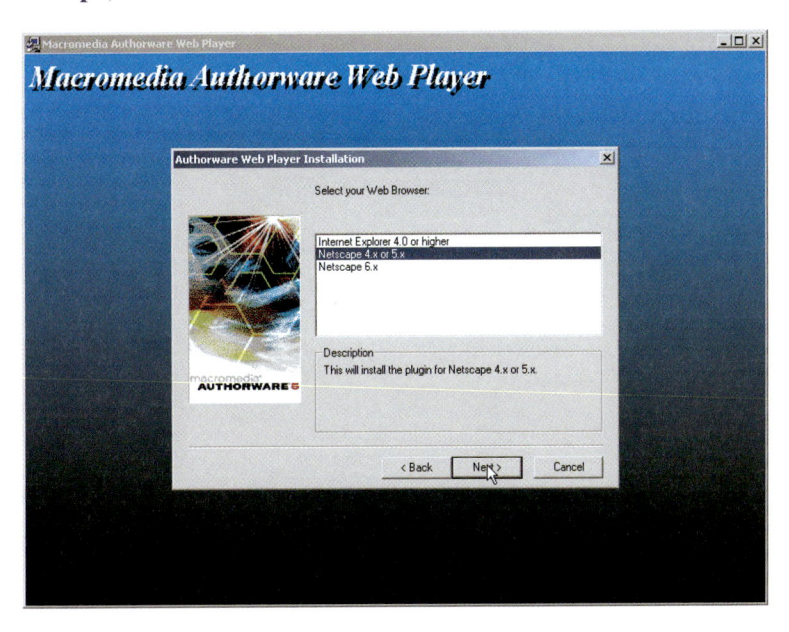

9. Now you will specify the path to the Netscape plug-in folder for your installation of Netscape.

Web Only Access (Cont'd)

10. If the default path that comes up is not correct for your installation, you can click on **Browse** to find the correct folder.

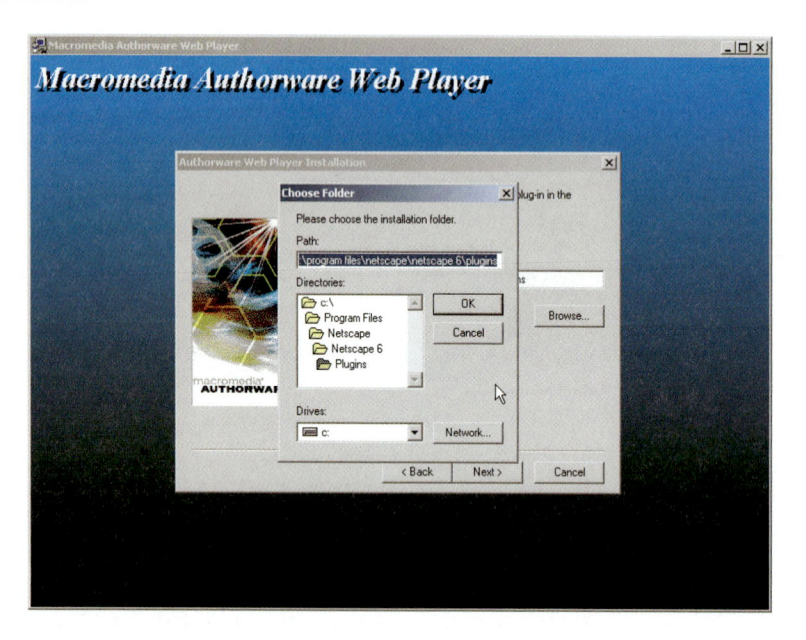

11. When the path is correct, click on **Next**.

12. You will see a status bar go across your screen to show you the progress of the installation.

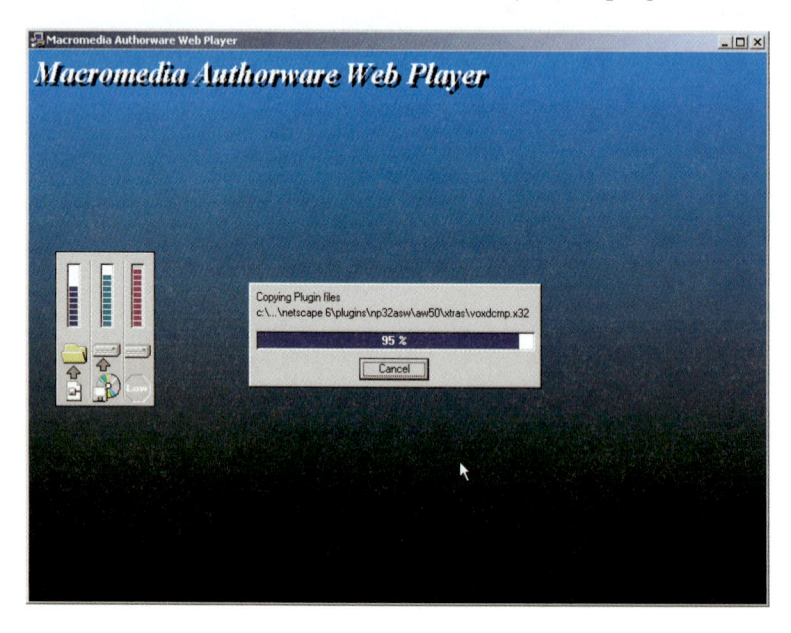

14

Web Only Access (Cont'd)

13. Finally, when the install is complete click on **Finish**.

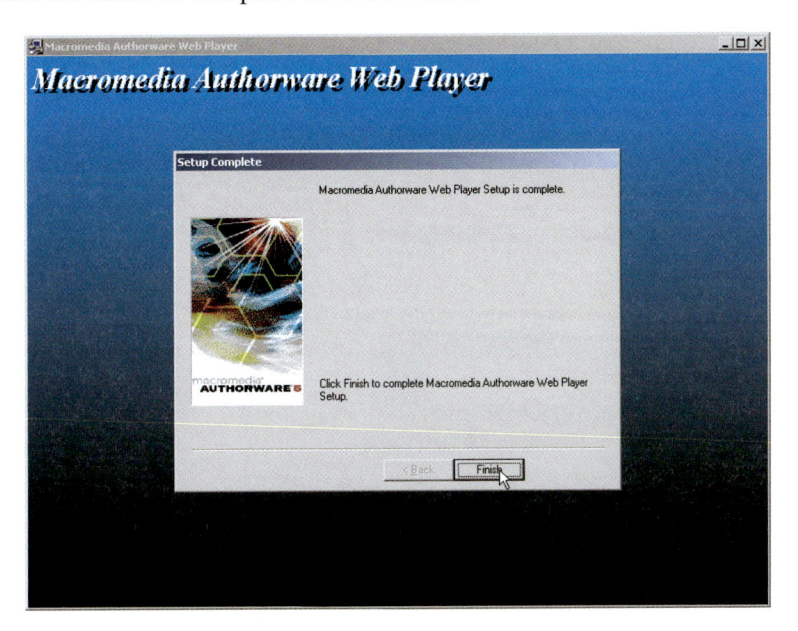

14. You are now ready to log into the program to begin your training or testing.

❖❖❖

Logging into to Train & Assess IT for the first time

If you were instructed to self-register into the program, you will need to follow the self-registration procedure below.
If you were NOT instructed to self-register, please see Registering with an Assigned Student Account on page 19.

❖ REGISTRATION PROCEDURE

Student Self-Registration

The Train & Assess IT site has a student self registration process. You will need two items to register:
- the 16 digit access code / pin code on the front of this booklet. _____
- Course ID provided by instructor. _____

Let's get started:

Web Only Access (Cont'd)

1. Go to: **http://www.phgenit.com**. You will see the **Sign In** screen shown here.

2. Click **New User** to sign in as a new student self-registering for the course.

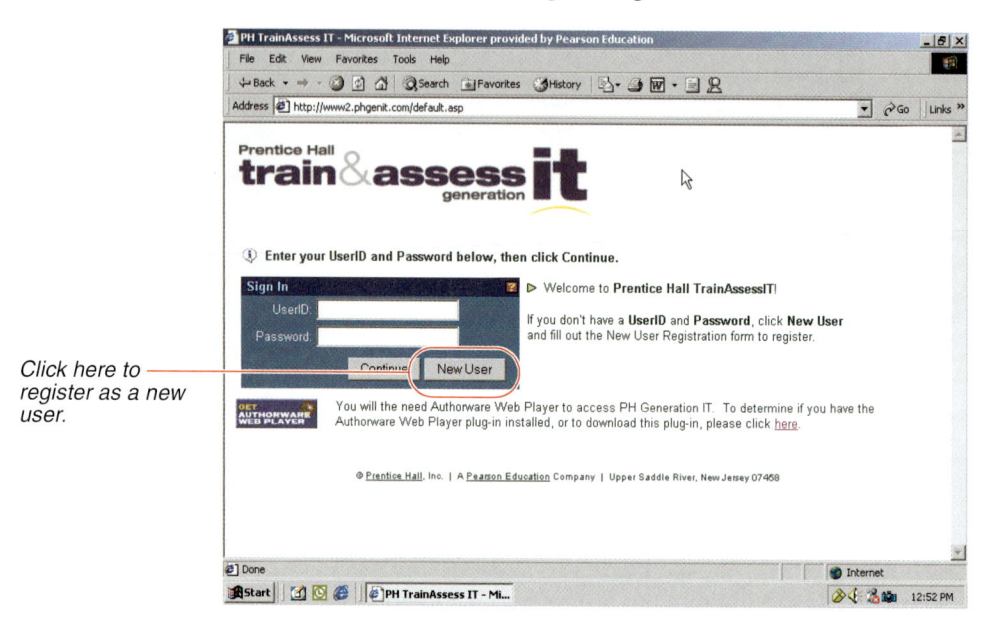

Click here to register as a new user.

3. You will now see a **New User Registration** screen. Fill in all the fields, creating your own unique UserID and password that you will use to log into Train & Assess IT in the future. You will need to fill in the Course/Section Code provided by your professor or instructor, and your 16 part Access Code / pin code. You can type the letters in upper case or lower case. All fields, including e-mail address, are required.

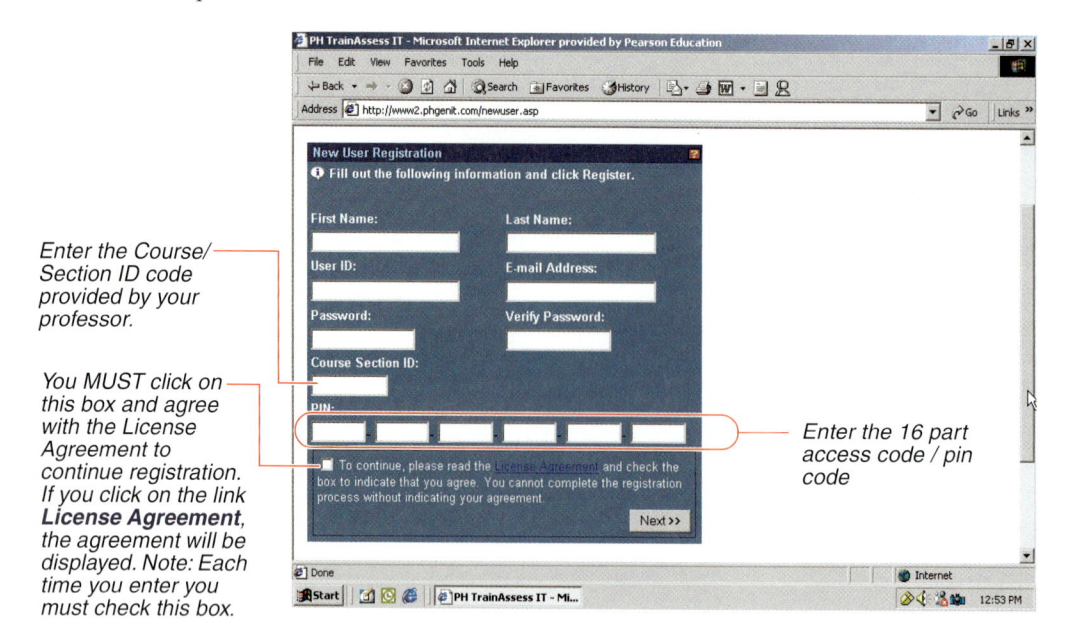

Enter the Course/Section ID code provided by your professor.

*You MUST click on this box and agree with the License Agreement to continue registration. If you click on the link **License Agreement**, the agreement will be displayed. Note: Each time you enter you must check this box.*

Enter the 16 part access code / pin code

16

Web Only Access (Cont'd)

4. Click on **Next** at the bottom of the page to proceed.

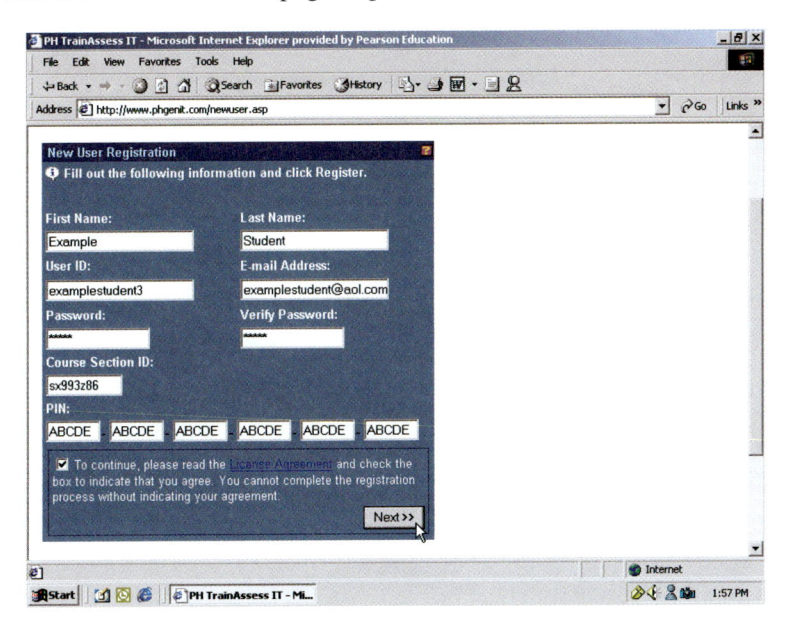

5. The next screen displays the user name you entered and the group you joined. It gives you the option to **Print** this information. It is a good idea to print this screen in case you forget your user name. Click on the **Register** button after you have printed this screen.

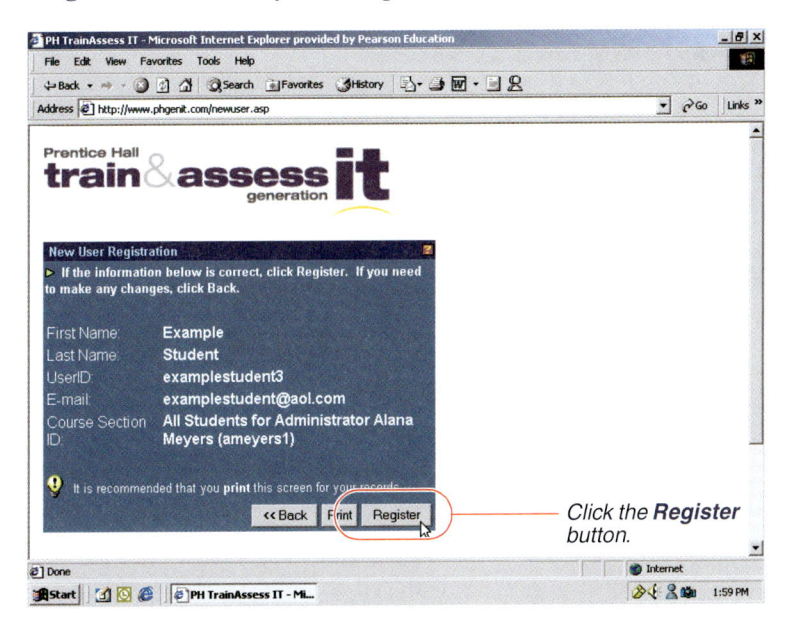

*Click the **Register** button.*

Web Only Access (Cont'd)

6. If you get the Internet Security warning below, click on **Yes** to successfully complete the registration process.

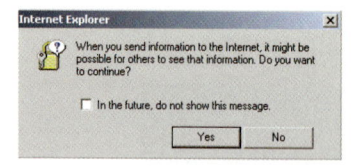

7. Following the above message you will get the warning below. ** You must click on **Yes** to successfully complete the registration process, otherwise you will void your current 16 part access code/ pin code and you will need a new one to register again.**

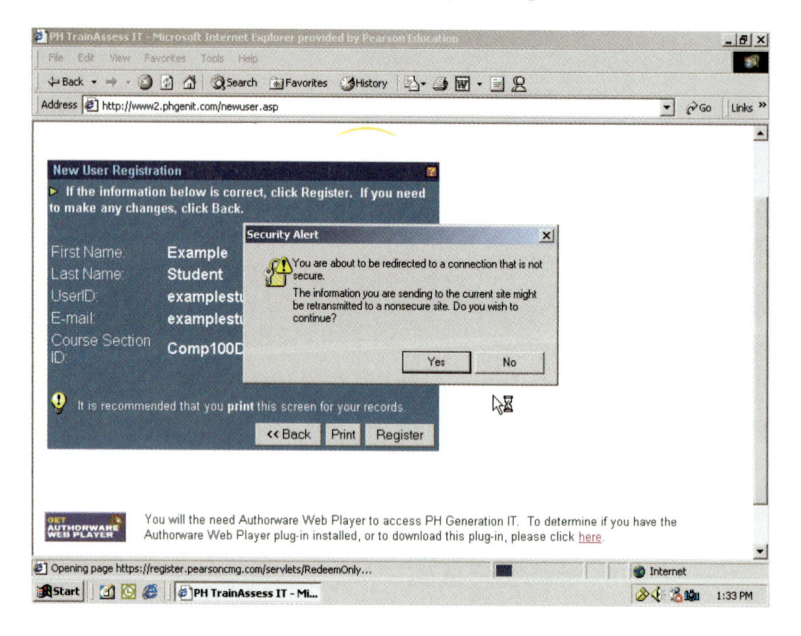

8. Congratulations! You are successfully logged in and registered!

Web Only Access (Cont'd)

9. The next time you return to Train & Assess IT, your log in experience will be slightly different.

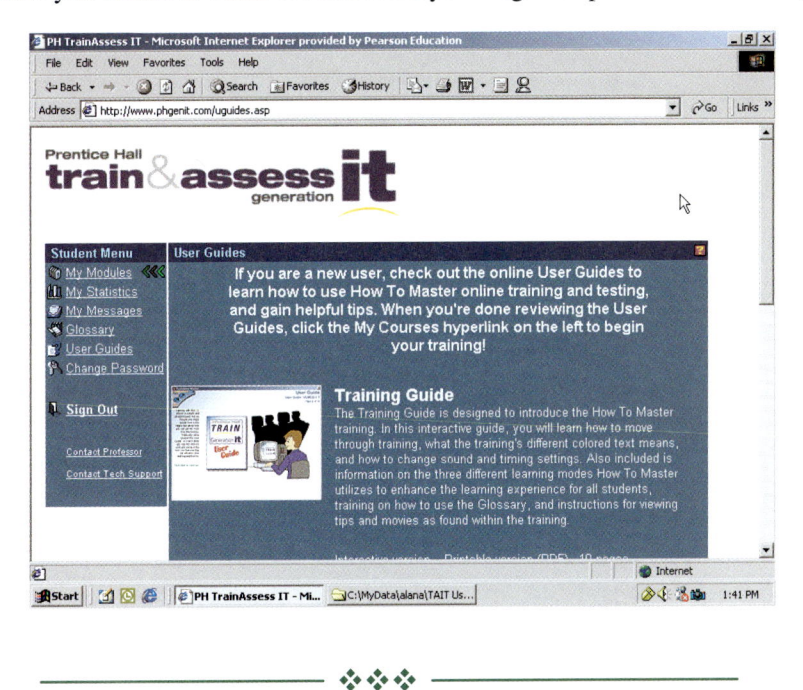

❖ REGISTRATION PROCEDURE

Registering with an Assigned Student Account

The Train & Assess IT site has a student account activation process.
You will need two items to register:
* the 16 digit access code / pin code on the front of this booklet. _____
* user id and password provided by instructor. _____

Keep your password in a safe place.
Let's get started:

　　　1. Go to: **http://www.phgenit.com.**

　　　2. You will see the **Sign In** screen shown as follows.

　　　3. Enter in the **UserID** and **Password** assigned to you by your professor/instructor.

19

Web Only Access (Cont'd)

4. Click on **Continue**.

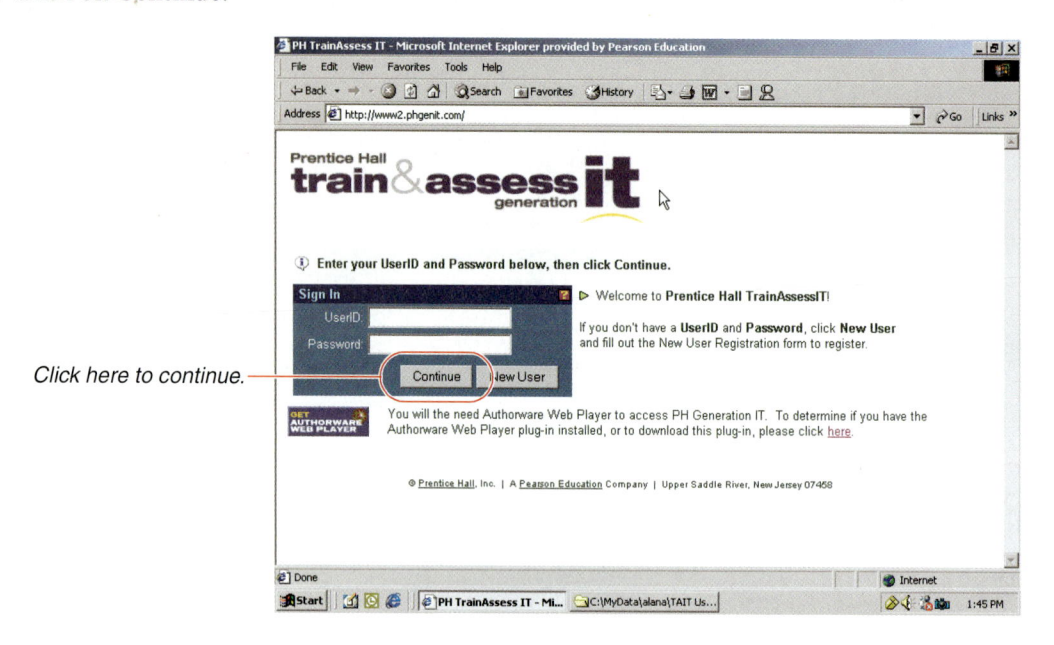

   Click here to continue.

5. Next you will be prompted with the **SMS Code Registration** screen. Enter in your 16 part Access Code / pin code. You can type the letters in upper case or lower case.

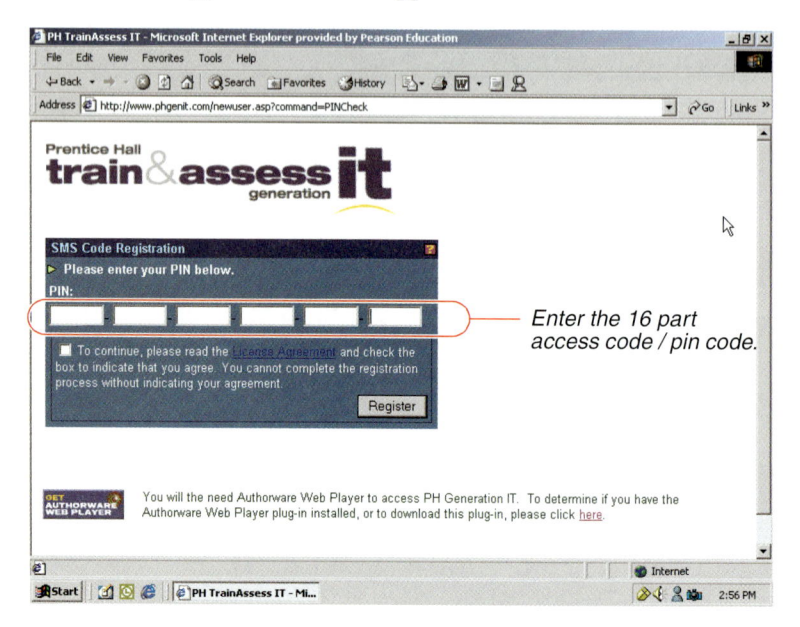

   Enter the 16 part access code / pin code.

Web Only Access (Cont'd)

6. Be sure to check the box next to the license agreement to accept it. You can view the agreement by clicking on **License Agreement**.

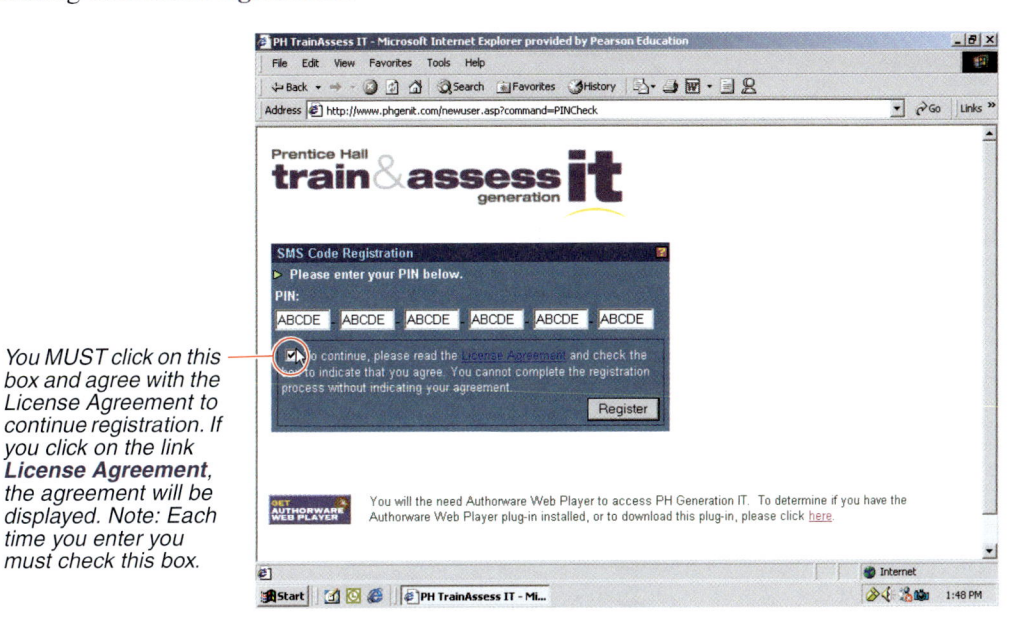

*You MUST click on this box and agree with the License Agreement to continue registration. If you click on the link **License Agreement**, the agreement will be displayed. Note: Each time you enter you must check this box.*

7. Click on **Register** to continue with the registration process.

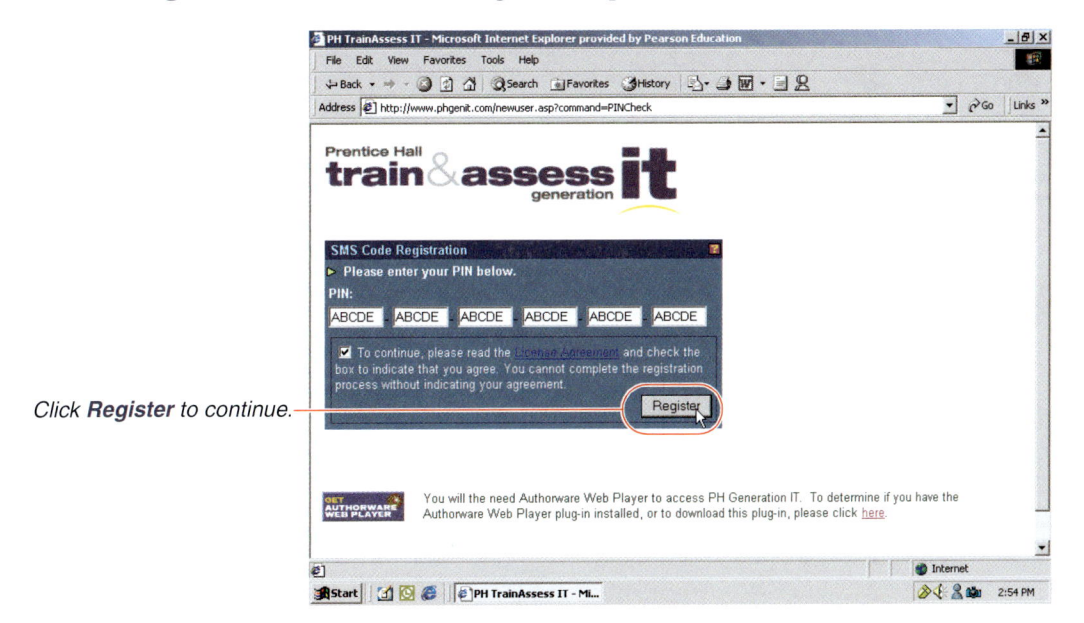

*Click **Register** to continue.*

Web Only Access (Cont'd)

8. If you get the Internet Security warning below, click on **Yes** to successfully complete the registration process.

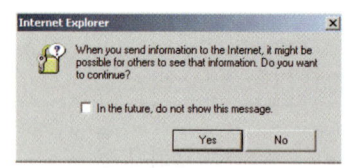

9. Following the above message you will get the warning below. You must click on **Yes** to successfully complete the registration process, otherwise you will void the current 16 part access code/pincode and will need a new one to register.

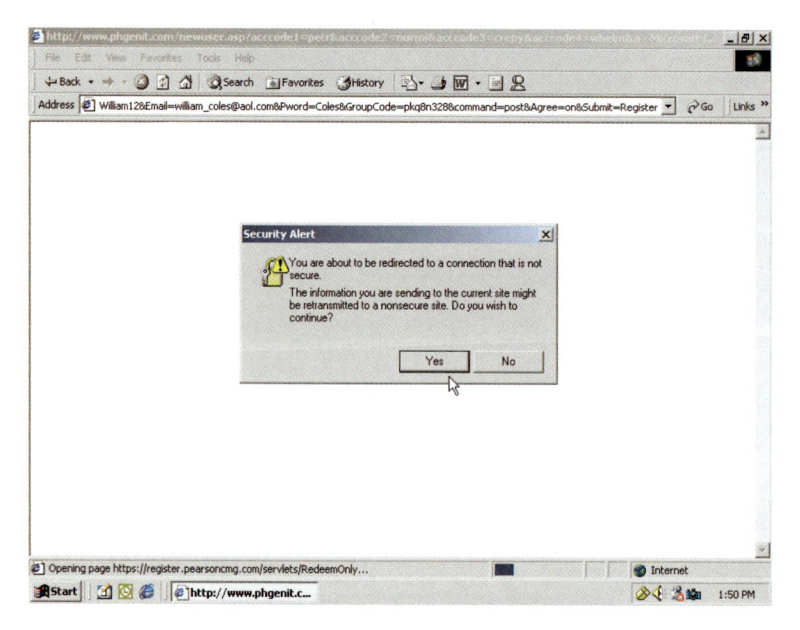

10. Congratulations! You are successfully logged in and registered!

Navigating Around Train & Assess IT

Train & Assess IT Main Menu

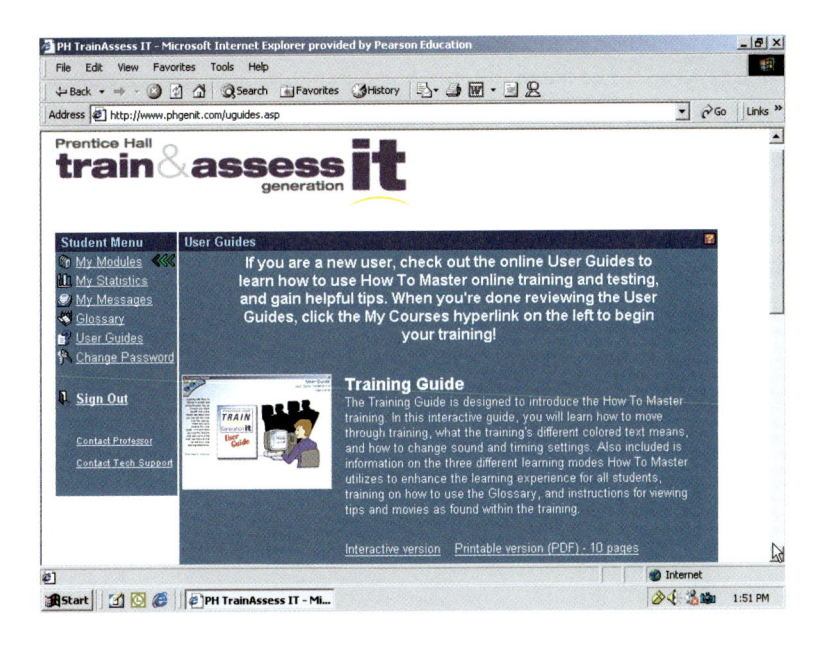

User Guides

There are several printable guides for users included in Train&Assess IT - a Training Guide, a Testing Guide and a Student Guide. If you are a new user, check out the online User Guides to learn how to use the training and testing sides of the program, alone with helpful hints. Click on the USER GUIDE option under the student menu to view or print out each guide.

- **Training Guide**

In this interactive guide, you will learn how to move through training, what the training's different colored text means, and how to change sound and timing settings. Also included is information on the different learning modes Train & Assess IT utilizes to enhance the learning experience for all students, training on how to use the Glossary, and instructions for viewing tips and movies found within the training.

- **Testing Guide**

In this interactive guide, you will learn about the six different types of questions found within the tests, as well as tips on how to answer each type of question. This guide also provides information on how to review the list of topics you are going to be tested on, as well as how to navigate through an exam. Lastly, the guide explains the evaluation information on the Student Information page, which appears at the end of a test.

Train & Assess IT Main Menu (Cont'd)

- **Student Guide**

The Student Guide is similar to most online help guides. It contains important information for students on how to view available modules, training statistics, and messages from their professor. Students can also learn to use the glossary and change their passwords. The Student Guide also explains how to sign out of Train & Assess IT when training or testing is complete, as well as how to contact the professor for additional help.

My Modules

This is where your training and testing modules will be located. When looking for assigned training or testing assignments, Click on **My Modules**.

My Statistics

This is where you will find the results of how you did on the assigned tests and training modules. Click on **My Statistics**.

My Messages

This is where you will go for e-mail messages to and from your instructor. Click on **My Messages**.

Glossary

Confused on a term used in either the training or testing portion of this program? To find a definition of a term, click on the glossary to search by name or even by first letter of the word you need a definition for. Click on **Glossary**.

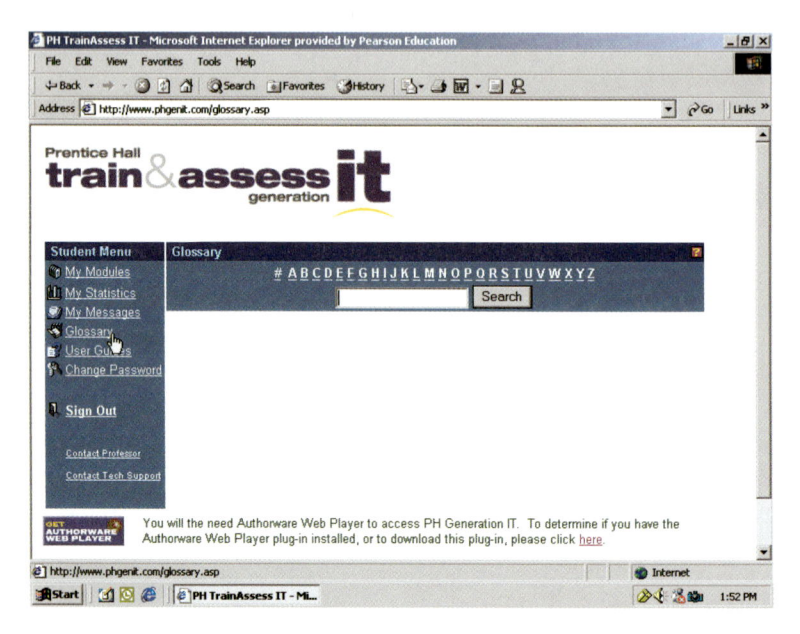

Train & Assess IT Main Menu (Cont'd)

Change Password

At anytime, as a user of Train & Assess IT, you have the ability to change your password. Click on **Change Password**.

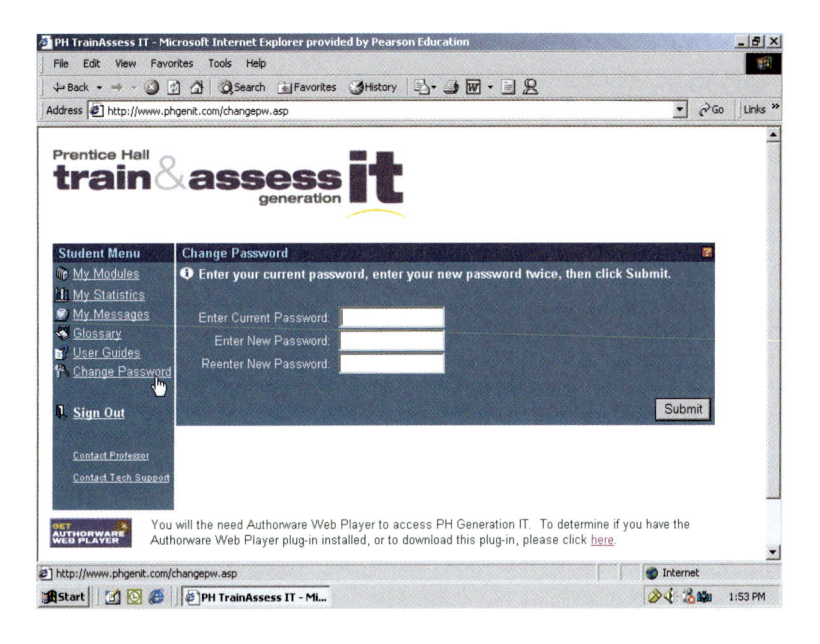

Sign Out

When you complete the lessons or tests assigned, or are simply ready to exit the program, you need to click on **Sign Out** to end your session.

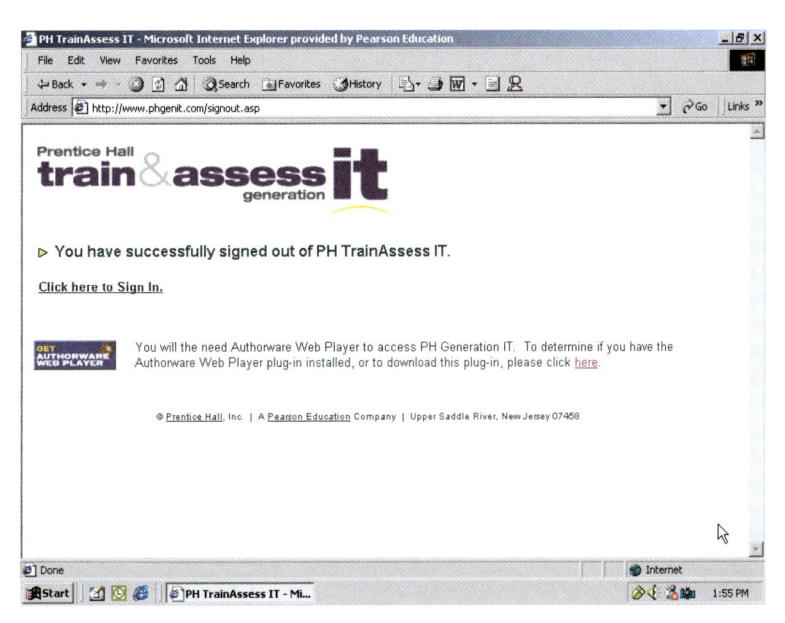

Train & Assess IT Main Menu (Cont'd)

Contact Professor

If your professor has enabled this feature, you will be able to send messages directly to them with questions. Click on **Contact Professor**

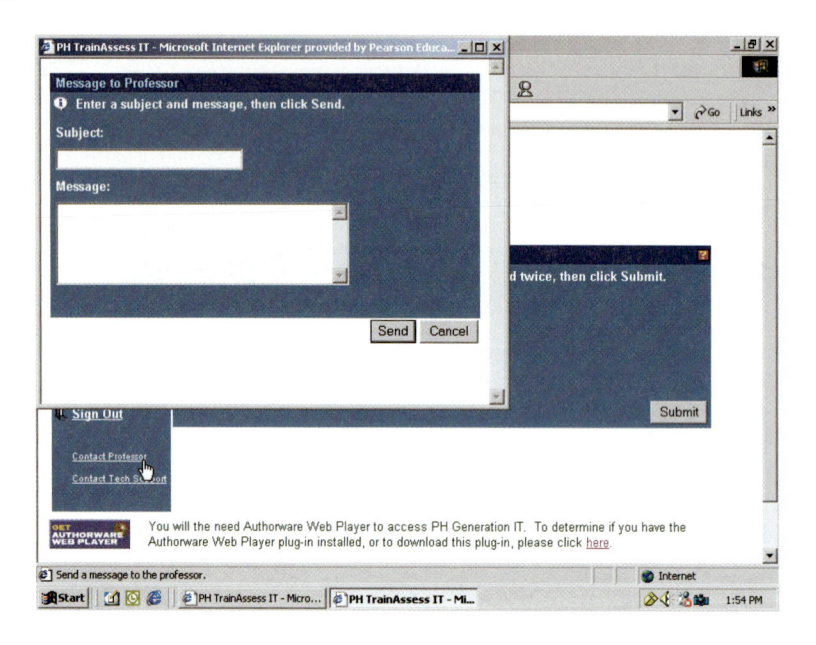

Contact Tech Support

At anytime you may e-mail direct to tech support. Some sample questions you would e-mail them for are: "Trouble downloading Authorware, Can't view the animations, Sound won't work, Can't find your course assignments, etc." They will e-mail you back and will help you continue forward in your learning on Train & Assess IT. Click on **Contact Tech Support**

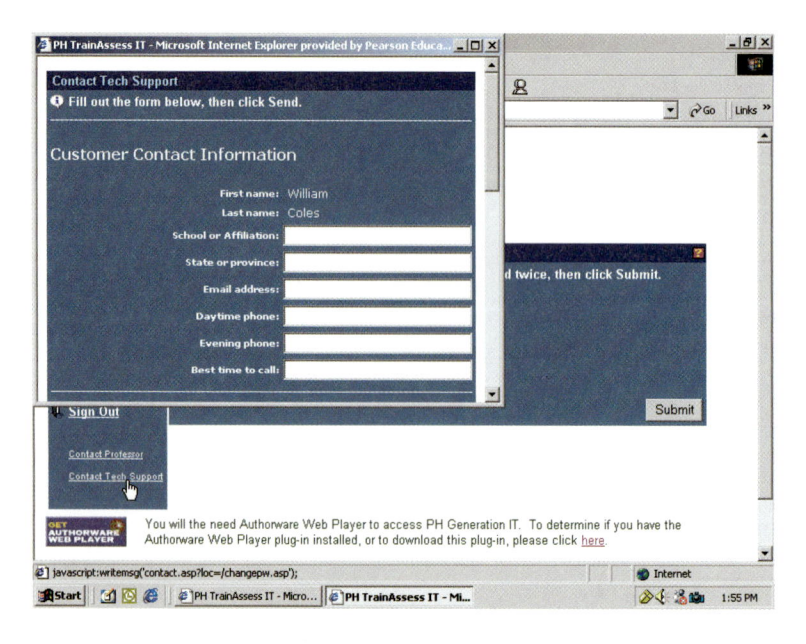

Training Walkthrough Overview

The following describes and shows how to begin a lesson, navigate and use the Train & Assess IT system. Please Note: Your training and assessment interface may appear slightly different depending on the version of Office you are using.

❖ PRODUCT WALKTHROUGH

Begin a Training Lesson

1. The training in Train & Assess IT is performance based and interactive. Once you begin a lesson you will read and/or listen to the words on the screen and complete the tasks when prompted. Many lessons open with a few informational slides followed by slides where you will be asked to perform tasks. Follow along and if you are stuck the program will prompt you and bring you to the next slide. To access your training lessons, click on **My Modules**, then select the assigned lesson.

Click on My Modules to access training lessons.

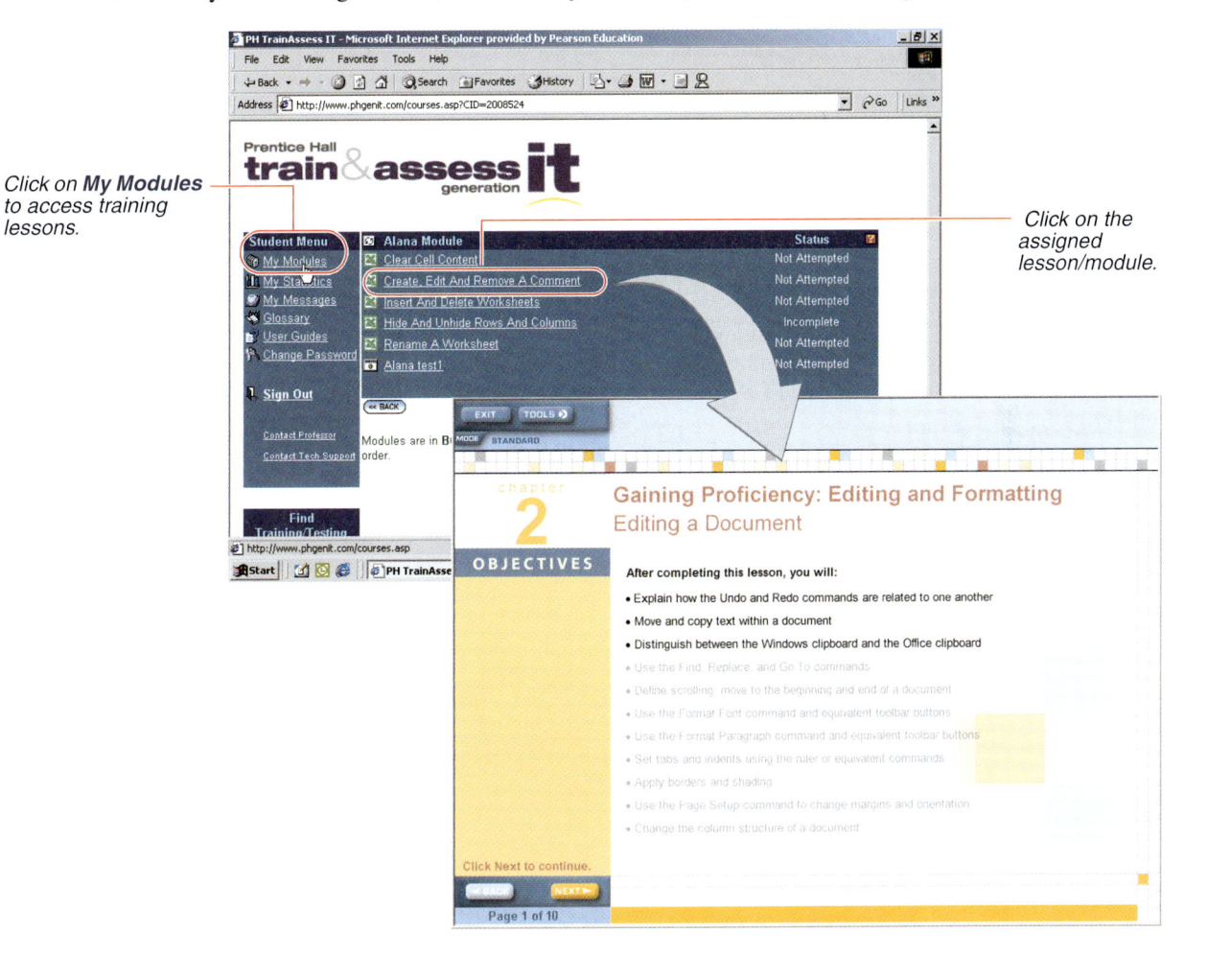

Click on the assigned lesson/module.

27

Training Walkthrough Overview (Cont'd)

❖ PRODUCT WALKTHROUGH

Navigate and Use Training

1. **Modes of Training**: You have an option for how you would like to work through the training. To select the mode of training you would like to work in, simply click on Mode to change the the setting. Each click will change the mode to one of the following:

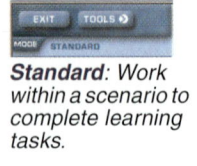

Standard: Work within a scenario to complete learning tasks.

Slide Show: Sit back and watch the training and review for an exam.

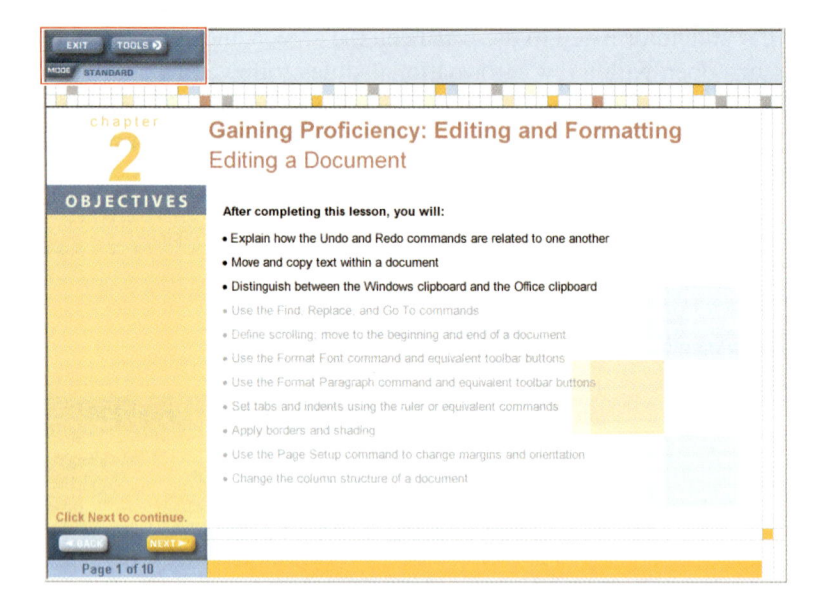

Training Walkthrough Overview (Cont'd)

2. To view the settings menu, click on **Tools** in the upper left-hand of the page and the following menu will be available. Select the setting you would like by clicking on one of the words.

3. The **Next** and **Back** buttons can be used to navigate through lessons. Click the **Exit** button when you have completed the training. If you have not completed the entire module, you can still exit and come back later to the exact place that you left off.

Settings: Turn the Sound On/Off, turn the narration On/Off, and change how quickly the pages turn in Slide Show Mode.

Tools

Exit: Click on Exit when you have completed the training. If you have not completed the entire module, you can still exit and come back later to the exact place you left off.

Next and Back Buttons: These help you navigate through the lesson.

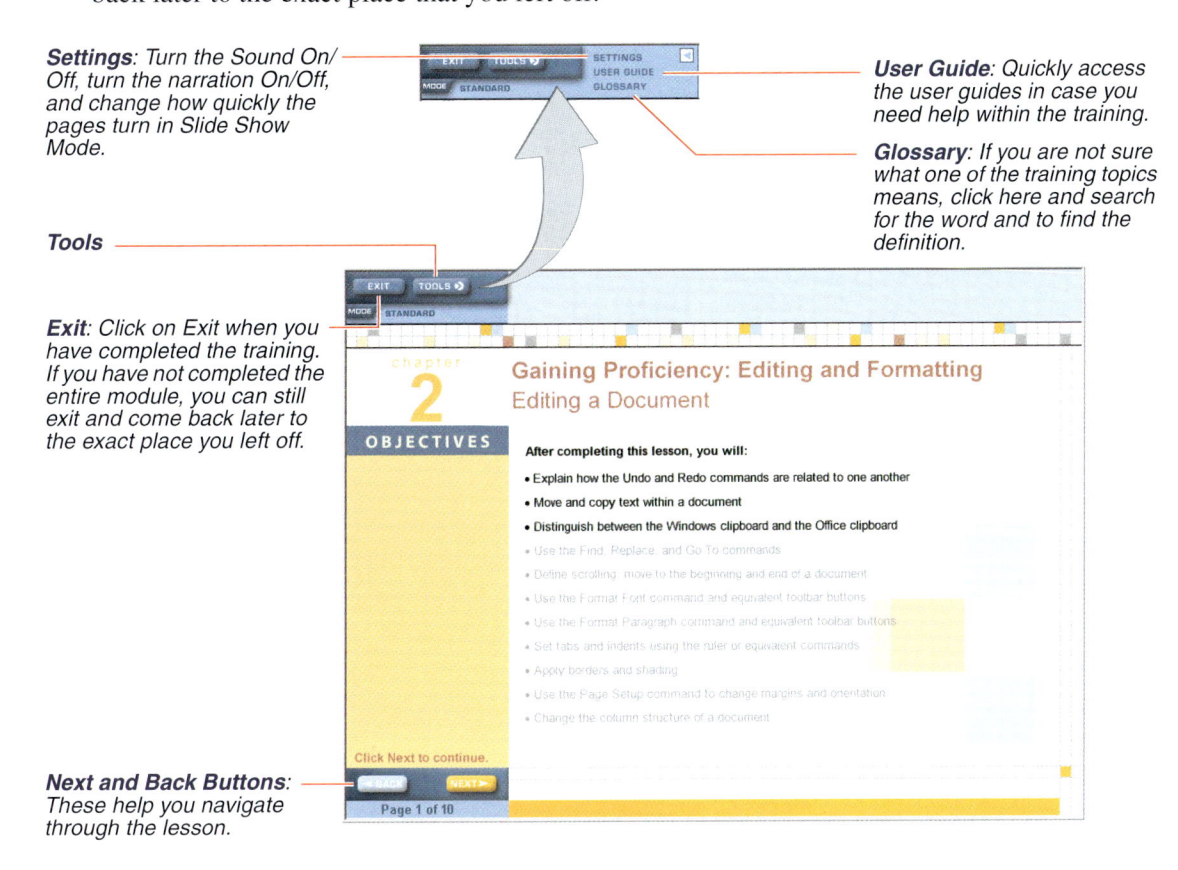

User Guide: Quickly access the user guides in case you need help within the training.

Glossary: If you are not sure what one of the training topics means, click here and search for the word and to find the definition.

Training Walkthrough Overview (Cont'd)

4. Blue bolded words within text areas are used to identify a link that when clicked will display the definition of the key term.

5. The **Status Box** in the lower left corner, will let you know how many slides you have completed and also how many you have left.

Click blue bolded words to display the definition of a key term.

Status Box: will let you know how many slides you have completed and how many you have left.

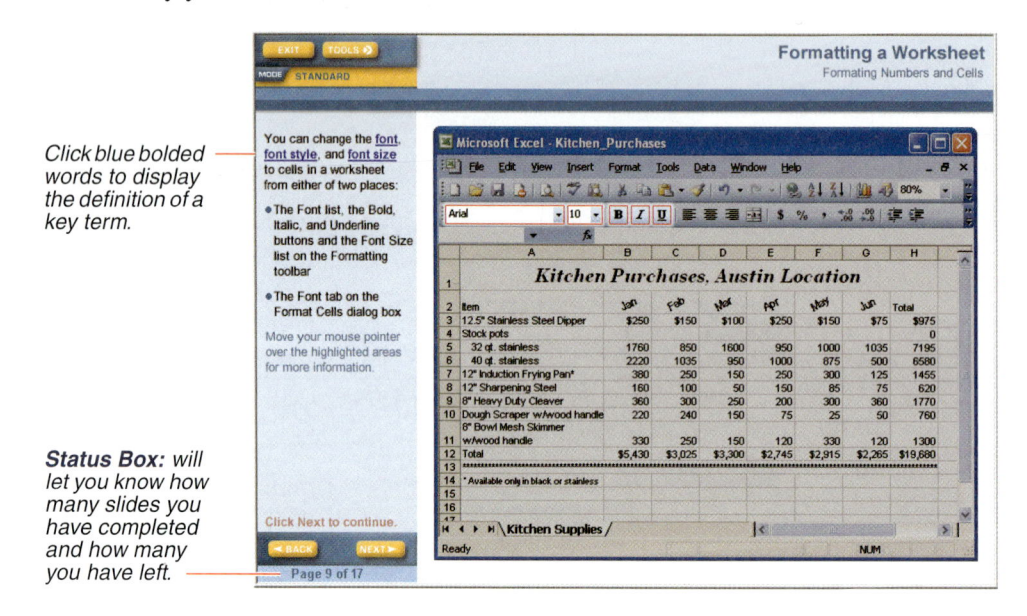

Assessment Walkthrough Overview

When taking a test in Train & Assess IT, you will be able to answer the questions by actually performing the tasks being asked. To complete the task "Bold the word Dog" (for example) you would highlight "Dog" and hit the Bold key on the toolbar. Once complete, the program will move forward to the next question. The program recognizes any way that you complete the task. Your professor has many options of how to administer the test, so frequently you will see the words 'if your professor has enabled these features,' it means that your professor has an option whether or not to make this available to you in a test. As a result, you may or may not see a particular feature.

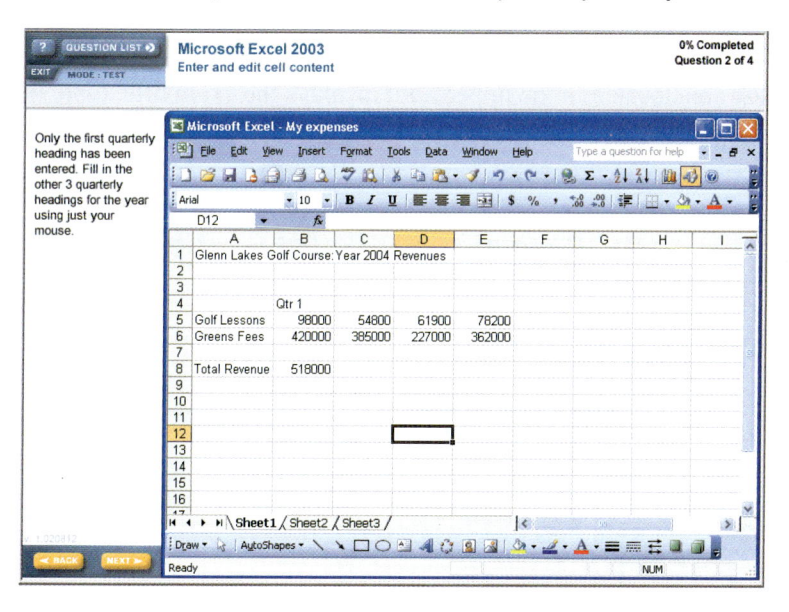

Assessment Walkthrough Overview (Cont'd)

❖ PRODUCT WALKTHROUGH

Navigate and Use Assessment

1. The **Navigation Box** located in the upper left contains the Question List and Exit buttons. Use the Next and Back buttons located in the lower left when you want to move ahead or go back to a question.

2. The **Test Question** area contains a question that directs you on what to do on the screen.

3. The **Status Box** area located in the upper right displays the exam title, topic being covered, % complete, question number you are on, and also the time you have spent (if the professor has enabled these features).

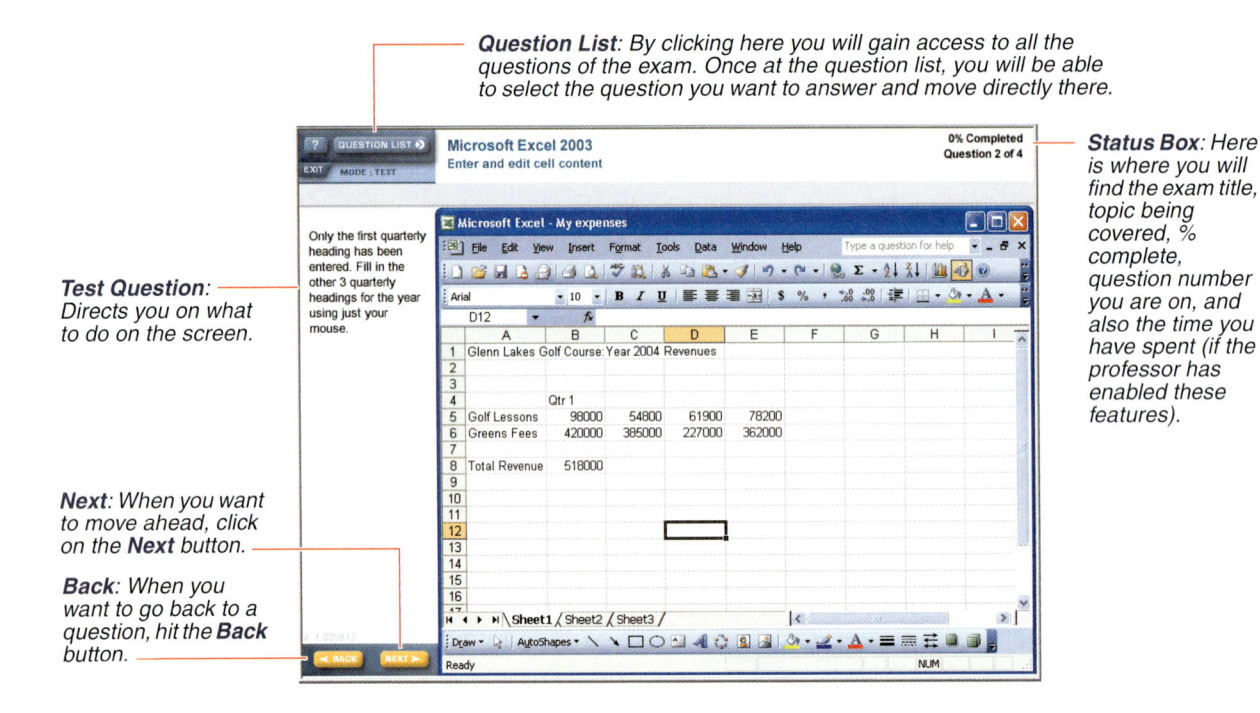

Question List: By clicking here you will gain access to all the questions of the exam. Once at the question list, you will be able to select the question you want to answer and move directly there.

Status Box: Here is where you will find the exam title, topic being covered, % complete, question number you are on, and also the time you have spent (if the professor has enabled these features).

Test Question: Directs you on what to do on the screen.

Next: When you want to move ahead, click on the **Next** button.

Back: When you want to go back to a question, hit the **Back** button.

Assessment Walkthrough Overview (Cont'd)

4. **Multiple Question Attempts**: Your professor may have enabled you to try a question more than once. If the computer shows you a message offering you the option to move on to the next question or try again, you can try the question once again.

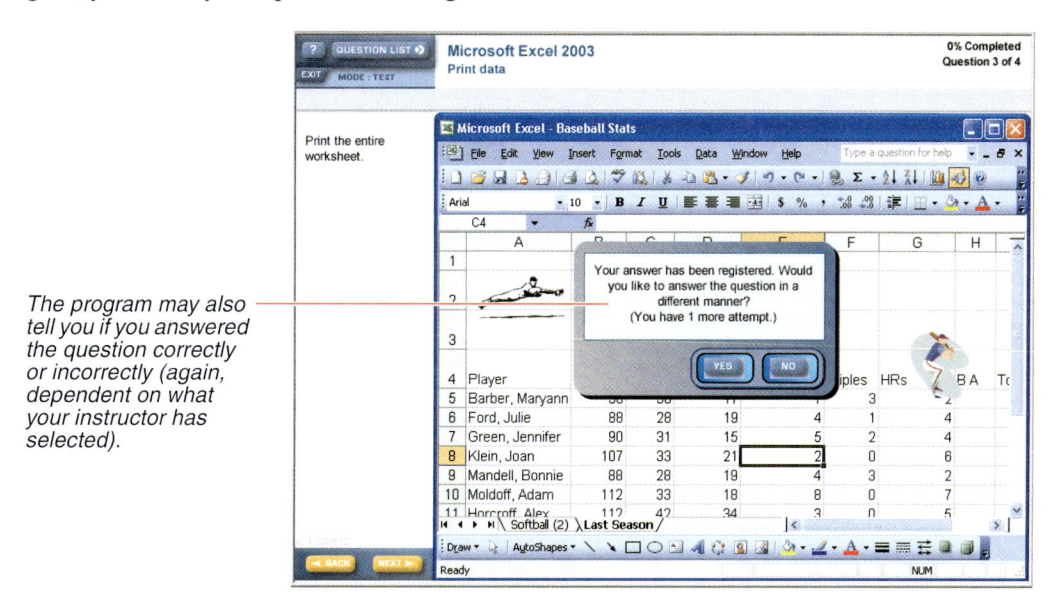

The program may also tell you if you answered the question correctly or incorrectly (again, dependent on what your instructor has selected).

5. **Exiting the Test**: Once you have completed the test, the program will ask you if you are complete. Click **Done** to exit the test, or **Redo Questions** to continue trying questions.

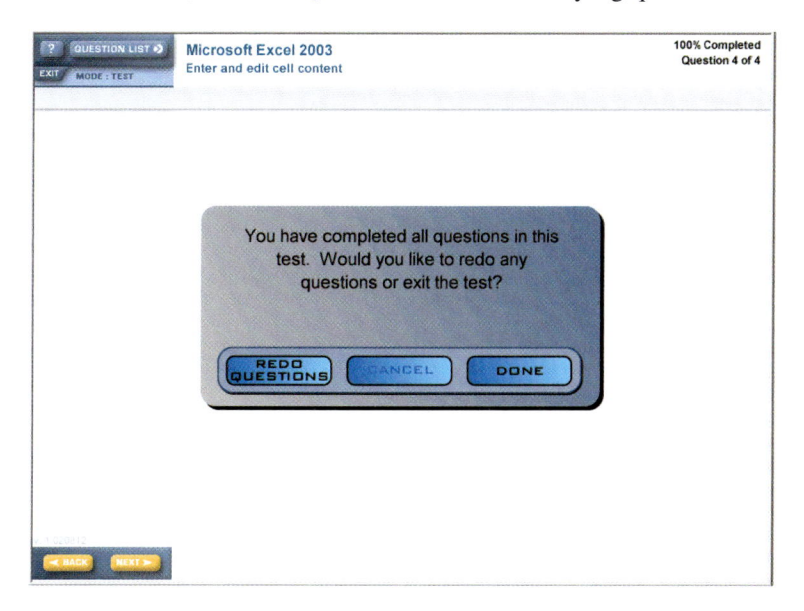

Assessment Walkthrough Overview (Cont'd)

6. **Immediate Feedback**: Once you exit the test, you may be able to see how you did on the test immediately (if your professor has enabled this feature). Our student report looks like this.

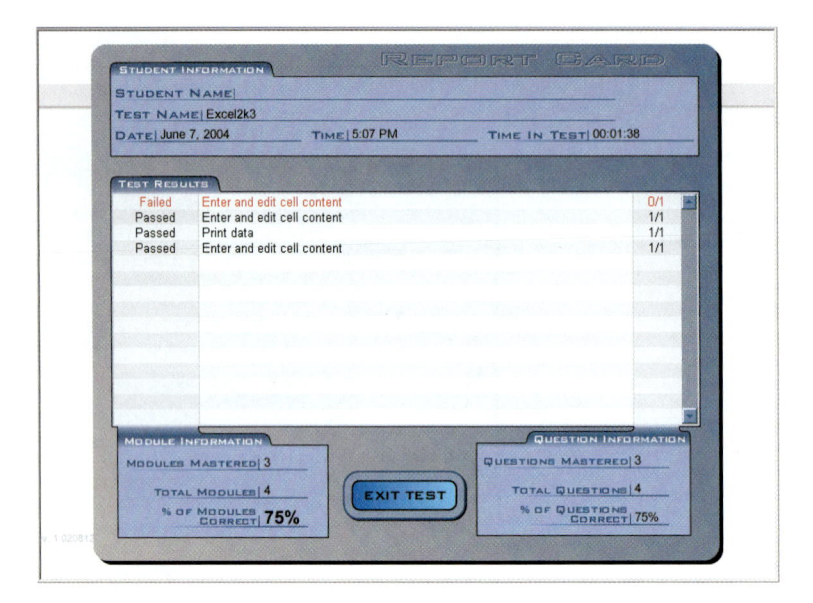

Assessment Walkthrough Overview (Cont'd)

7. **Check Results from the Main Menu**: Additionally, you can go to the main menu once you have completed your exam, and (if your professor has enabled these results) you will click on reports.

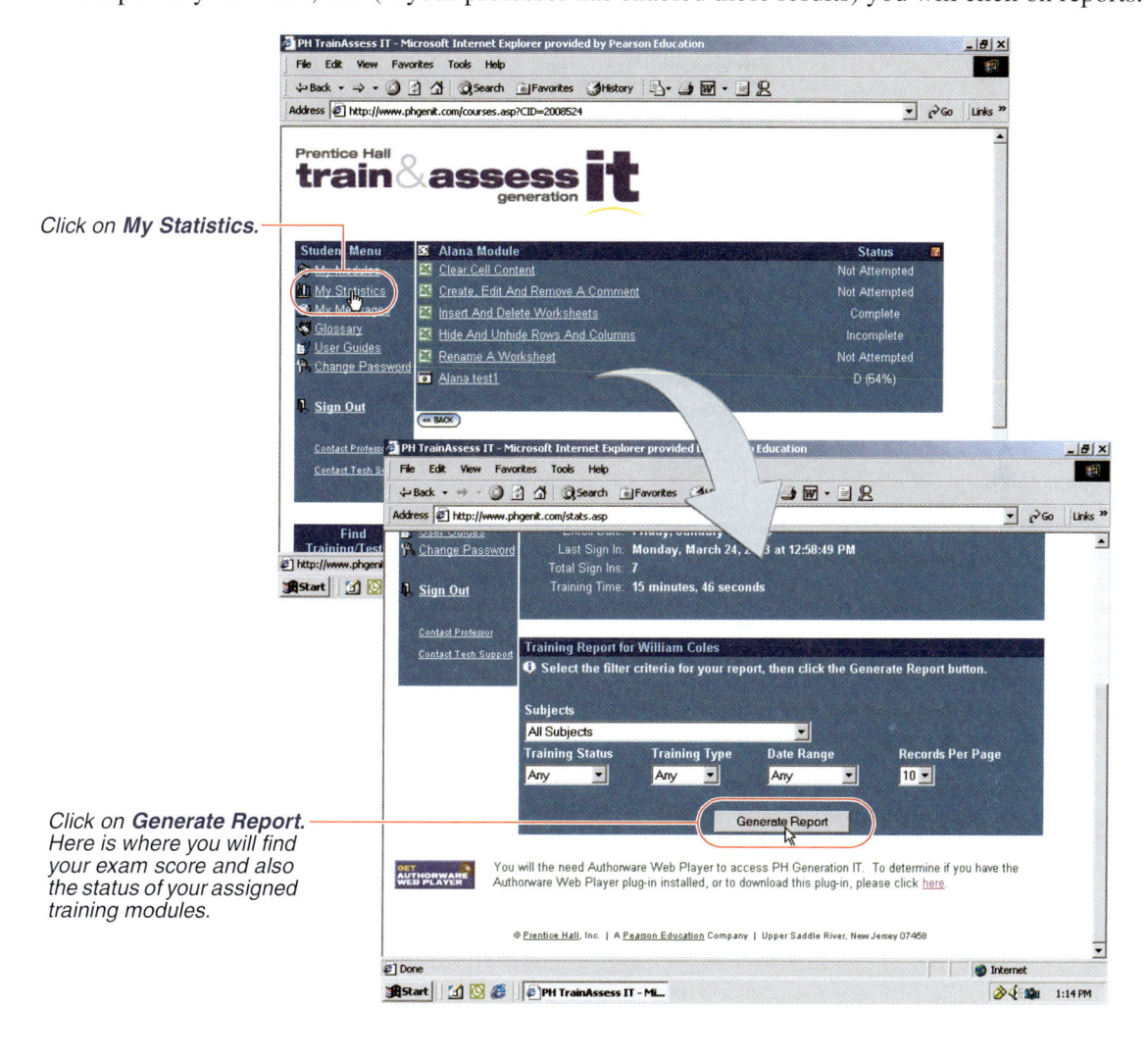

*Click on **My Statistics**.*

*Click on **Generate Report**. Here is where you will find your exam score and also the status of your assigned training modules.*

Tech Support

To contact technical support with questions, simply click on the **Contact Tech Support** link while signed into the program-as seen below:

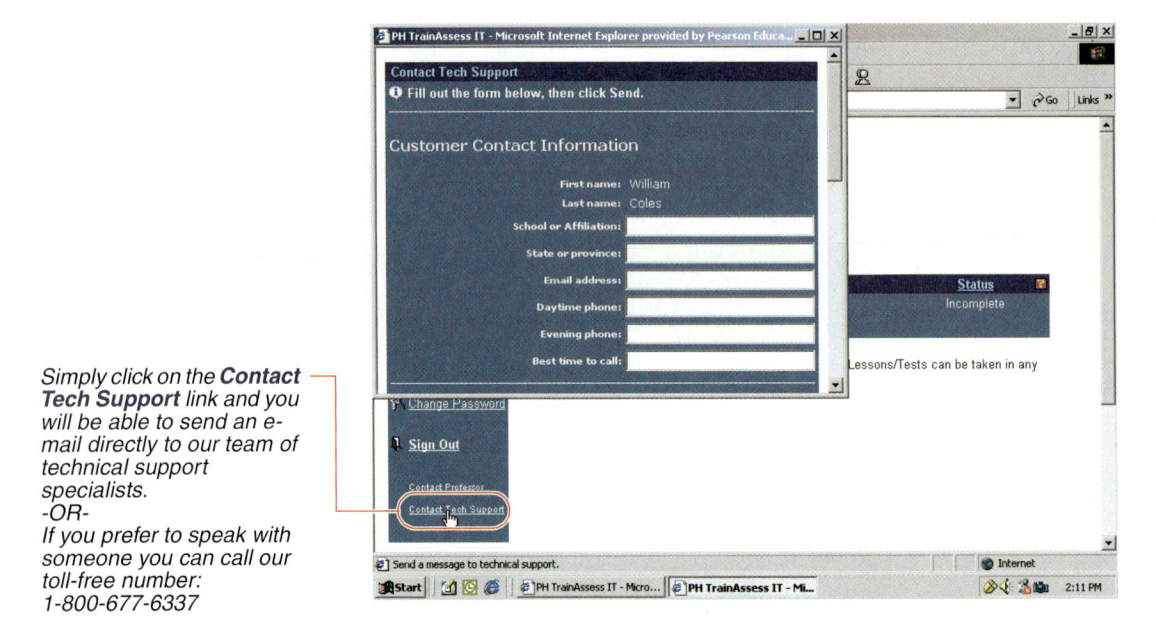

*Simply click on the **Contact Tech Support** link and you will be able to send an e-mail directly to our team of technical support specialists.*
-OR-
If you prefer to speak with someone you can call our toll-free number:
1-800-677-6337

Uninstalling the Partial Local Install CD

❖ INSTALL PROCEDURE

Uninstalling the Partial Local Install CD

1. To uninstall the Partial Local Install version of Train & Assess IT, you will need to go to the **Start Menu**. Click **Settings**. Click **Control Panel**.

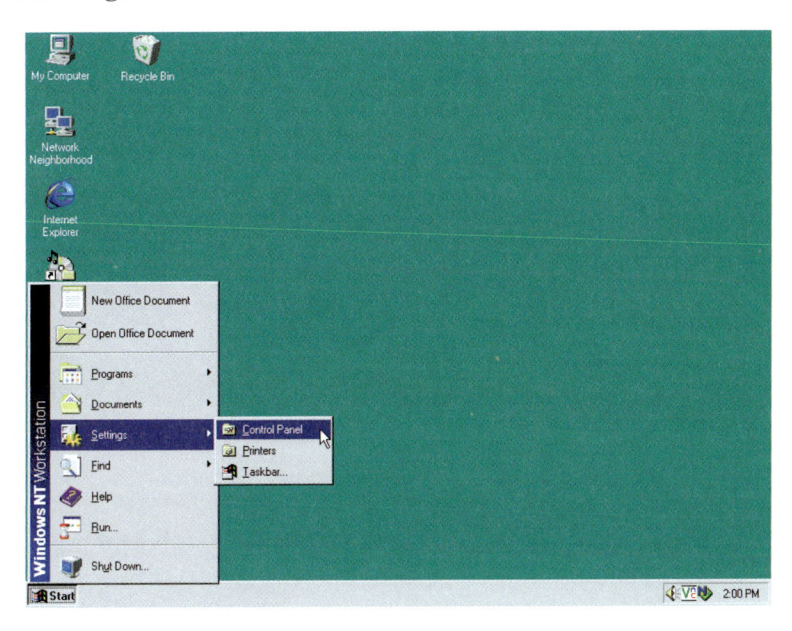

2. Click **Add/Remove Programs**.

Uninstalling the Partial Local Install CD (Cont'd)

3. Select PH Train and Assess Generation IT-part 1. Click **Change/Remove**.

4. Follow the wizard, selecting **Remove**.

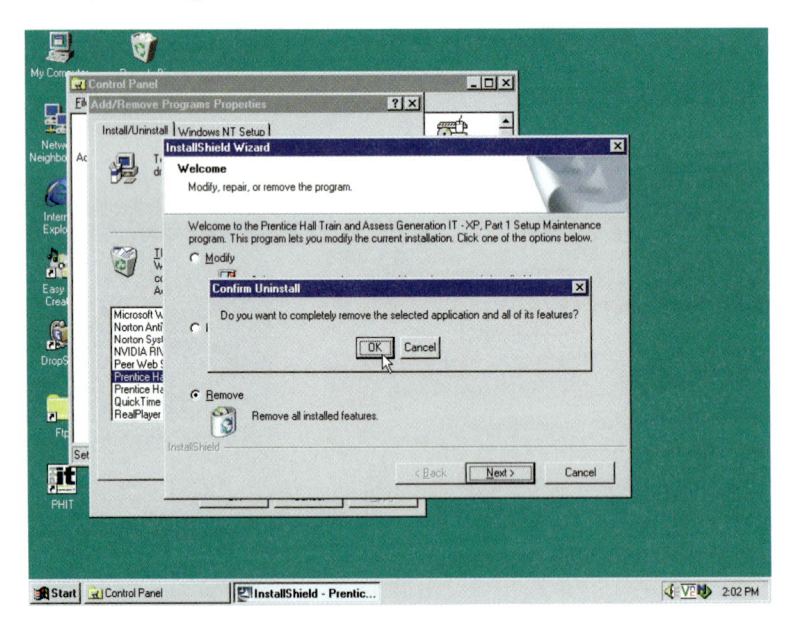

5. Click **OK**.

❖❖❖

The Train IT CD

If you want to do the training with no internet connection required, you can use the Train IT CD in this package. To begin, put the CD into the CD-ROM drive. The CD will start immediately (you do not need to install anything).

Although you do not need Authorware to run this CD, there is a download of this available if you wish to access the web only version of Train & Assess IT.